WAITING TO GO!

G-5861

Waiting to Go!

African American Church Worship Resources from Advent through Pentecost

James Abbington
and Linda H. Hollies

GIA Publications, Inc.
Chicago • www.giamusic.com

G-5861
Copyright © 2002
GIA Publications, Inc.
7404 S. Mason Ave., Chicago, IL 60638

www.giamusic.com

ISBN: 1-57999-149-1
Book layout and design: Robert Sacha
All rights reserved • Printed in the United States of America

"Let the Word of God dwell in you richly in all wisdom,
teaching and admonishing one another in psalms and hymns and spiritual songs,
singing with grace in your hearts to the Lord!"

—Colossians 3: 16 NIV

Table of Contents

Dedications and Acknowledgements ... 1

Introduction ... 3

About the Christian Year ... 4

About the Revised Common Lectionary ... 6

A Word about the Musical Selections ... 7

Christ the King Sunday ... 10

Thanksgiving ... 12

Advent ... 15

Christmastide ... 25

Epiphany ... 37

Lent ... 65

Holy Week ... 85

Easter ... 103

Ascension ... 118

Pentecost ... 123

A Worship Planning Worksheet ... 128

Appendix of Resources ... 115

Selected Bibliography ... 144

Dedications and Acknowledgements

This work is dedicated to every church musician, choir director, choir, singing group, and soloist who I have met and worked with over the years.

As a child, I remember the dedication of Molly Walker and Sally Clark. They "plunked" the old piano at the 17th Street Church of God in Christ where I was raised, and helped me to remember and come to love the old songs of the Church. As a young adult, I remember John Berry and Matthew Whittington, who gave us the sounds that assisted the choir in rendering anthems in grand style. As a pastor in training, I am appreciative of my mentor, Dr. Willie B. Clay, who had every choir: the Chancel, the Gospel, the Young Adult, the Inspirational, and the Youth choirs, sing every Sunday. He taught me how to richly feed every member of the congregation in song. That way, no one would have an excuse to stay home until his or her "favorite" choir sang! It's a lesson I yet value today.

As a United Methodist pastor, I have had the opportunity to work with some of the best in the music industry. I give God thanks for my first Minister of music, Diane Mitchell. Diane and the members of Praise fed my spirit every Sunday in a primarily Anglo congregation. The anointing of the Holy Spirit rests heavily and mightily upon this woman, and I thank God for putting her in my life. Linda Elliott, at my second charge, is another lover of music who can translate it beyond the page. Bobby Battle helped me to move my first Black congregation to the new innovation called the keyboard! And every Sunday, we sang *Speak to My Heart* before I preached. It was an awesome experience that brought deliverance to many souls. Thank you to Cynthia Wilson-Felder, Johnnetta Page, Jannette Chandler-Kotey and The Anointed Jackson Singers, along with my son, concert flautist Grelon Renard Everett, my brother, concert violinist Obed Shelton, and my daughters, Grian Hollies and Vera Riley, for always blessing me with their ministry of music.

I am not sure where the idea originated that sparked my interest in writing liturgies. However, I am sure that it was a gift from God to encourage the saints. It was from this writing venture that Dr. Melva Costen took note and made use of my work in her classes at The Interdenominational Theological Center. She introduced it to Dr. James Abbington, who called and asked if I would teach a class at Hampton. He and co-director, Royzell Dilliard allowed me a rare privilege, as both a female pastor and a non-Baptist, to interact with musicians from across the nation. This work is a direct result. My prayer is that it will assist musicians and choirs to better minister in their God given role of spreading the Living Word through song.

Because of my work at The Hampton Musician's Guild Workshop, I have been blessed to take some time and work with an awesome Baptist pastor, Derrick Lewis-Noble and Minister of Music, Lamar James and praise Leader, George Lowe at the New Hope Baptist Church in Grand Rapids, Michigan. Every worship experience is a life giving experience. I thank God for this unity in the Body of Christ. With you, I'm in the land of "wait" to see how God moves next! Until then, I'm praying for you and ask your prayers in return. Shalom! God's best shalom!

—Sista Linda H. Hollies

Acknowledgements

I received an anonymous email during the writing of this book that read, "I believe that friends are quiet angels who lift us to our feet when our wings have trouble remembering how to fly." While I have been unable to find the author of these profound words, I have borrowed them to express my sincere gratitude and appreciation for the "quiet angels" who have prayed, encouraged, and supported me during this endeavor.

I gratefully acknowledge my mother, Daisy Ann Barlow, and my father, Wilbur J. Abbington, Sr.; my Shaw University colleagues and administrators, Dr. Ernest L. Pickens, Dr. Lillie M. Boyd, and Dr. Gale Isaacs; my students, Antwan Lofton, Rashaan Jacobs, and Jason Brooks; my secretary, Mrs. Mildred Hooker; my "little" brother, Travis Morris; and Mr. Don Walston, whose example of generosity and unconditional support for my musical efforts are unparalleled.

Language fails to express my heartfelt appreciation to all of you who have "lifted me to my feet" on those occasions when I had "trouble remembering how to fly."

A special thanks to my GIA family: Ed Harris, Bob Batastini, Alec Harris, Robert Sacha, Denise Wheatley, Vicki Krstansky, Jeff Mickus, Kelly Dobbs Mickus, and all the rest, for your kindness and unswerving support, competence, and efficiency.

What can I say about Sista Linda? You have become my sista, friend, counselor, colleague, and now, co-author. I thank God for sending you my way.

—James Abbington

Introduction

Nikki Giovanni wrote a poem that says, "All I ever do is sit and wait!" Waiting is familiar to People of color. We waited in slave castles for those ships, which would set sail with us as the precious cargo. We waited for the passage of those same ships across dangerous waters. We waited as hunger, humiliation, and even death stalked the hulls where we were stored. We were forced to wait upon auction blocks to be sold as animals. We waited for emancipation as we labored to make ourselves at home in a foreign land. And, we waited for freedom. We continue to wait. Nikki's words are so true and appropriate... "All I ever do is sit and wait!"

Although waiting is not one of our favorite things to do, we have grown accustomed to waiting. Our national dislike of waiting has brought about drive through lines, ATM machines, e-mail and instant messages, and every type of quick fix food and even "get rich quick" scams! Yet, God requires that we continue to wait. Certain things will not hurry. Certain seasons will not be rushed. Certain journeys require the long way. There are no short cuts. So, God forces us to wait. For waiting is part of God's master plan for life.

The mystery of Advent is that we are forced to wait. Advent signals days of preparing for the birth of the Christ. From the first or second Sunday after Thanksgiving until Christmas Eve, the Christian world is on watch, so we wait on the arrival of The Holy One. Many traditions honor this waiting time by lighting an Advent Candle Wreath. The wait is on. For the next four weeks, we sit. We wait. The Christ is coming. His mother, Mary, is pregnant! We should be pregnant, too!

The candles are purple or blue sometimes a rose colored one is lit on the third Sunday to signal our joy that the day is drawing near. They are lit to indicate that the regal one of glory will soon be arriving. It's not until Christmas Day that we light the huge center candle, which is white and called The Christ Candle. If there is a Christmas Eve worship, it is not appropriate to light that candle until after midnight. We cannot hurry the birth of Jesus Christ. It was both a natural and supernatural event that took time. All the world could do was sit and wait. A pregnancy requires nine months of waiting. Our time is a short wait.

Advent is about waiting, watching, anticipating, expecting, looking forward to and preparing our hearts to be clean mangers for the coming birth. Far too many are continuing to say, like the InnKeeper, "No room." In our congregations, there are too many who want the Child to come to a "room" not clean enough to house him! Therefore, Advent is our time to get ready. For like Mary, we ought be pregnant and ready to give birth to new ways in which to spread the message of Jesus Christ in our world.

The ancient text of the Evangelist Luke calls us to, "Prepare the way for the Lord, make straight paths for him," (Luke 3:4). This says that we are not ready! But, we must get ready. Thank God for waiting time. Thank God that Christ is not about to crack the sky, sound the trumpet, and find too many of us left behind! We want to run head long, quick, fast, and in a hurry to get to the festive season of Christmas. However, since it did take Jesus forty-two generations to get to us in human form, surely we can prepare for four weeks to celebrate his birth.

Yes! We are forced to wait. And in our waiting, we consider our ways. In our waiting, we repent of our sin. In our waiting, we re-connect with our community. In our waiting, we make room in our busy lives for others. In our waiting, we prepare to receive the Host of Heaven who comes to tabernacle to feed us with The Bread of Heaven, which satisfies our hungry, waiting souls.

If there is any one nation that knows the importance of waiting, it is the Black Church. Watch Night worships began as groups of us got together to "watch the days of slavery" disappear with the signing of the Emancipation Proclamation document. We were ready to go!

People were not always certain of their new destinations, but they gathered together in preparation to go to a new place, a new freedom, new beginnings. Advent prepares us for the One who was born to die and give us an Easter to celebrate. Advent helps us to walk the Lenten journey to Calvary with Jesus. Then Advent gives us the required spiritual muscles to wait for the arrival of The Holy Spirit at Pentecost! Pentecost is our signal to go! We are to go, at Pentecost, into all the world and tell them about the Savior who came to send us out to reach them in his name!

Waiting to Go! is a resource book, a read-to-use book, and a workbook designed to help congregational worship leaders and musicians with their ministries. Classical scriptures, held sacred down through the centuries, will be offered as guides to The Christian Year. Appropriate music, hymns, gospel, Anthems, traditional, contemporary, and especially that provided by African American artists will be uplifted. Sermon suggestions will assist in tying together the theological themes that arise between Hebrew Scripture, Psalms, and Gospel passages. This book will become an invaluable guide that will compliment those traditions that are sacred to your particular congregation. Let the Holy Spirit minister through these suggestions as we each prepare, *Waiting to Go!*

About the Christian Year

"In the beginning, God created...." God's Story of interaction with the created world began, and before too long of a period of time, the People sinned! The People needed a way out of the separation that was created between them and God. So, God promised that a method of redemption would be made. God gave Eve the assurance that "her seed" would come to bruise the head of the evil one. In chapter three of "The Beginning," we find the first mention of The Advent of Jesus Christ. The word *adventus* means *to come*. Advent is the opening season of The Christian Year. We stop our busyness and begin to wait intentionally for The Christ who comes.

God stepped out into the deep gloom and chaos of nothingness and pushed back boundaries, established limits to disorder, and broke into the dismal state with light. It was the first day of creation. Advent comes to break into our everyday chaotic routines like a winter lent. It is a season that calls us to push back our spiritual limits, to call forth order into our out-of-control lives, and begin a deliberate inward and forward look for Jesus Christ; The Light of The World!

On the second day of Creation, God separated the waters and placed an expanse between the heavens and the earth. The season of *Christmas* comes as a reminder that a bit of heaven has condescended to earth in the physical presence of Jesus Christ, The Only Begotten Son of God. Jesus was enfolded in the embryonic water fluids of Mary's womb. On the night that those separating waters broke, angelic heralds were dispatched with calls for earthly beings to participate in the new day that was approaching. Heavenly angels sang songs of praise the night Jesus was born. And his birth certainly brought joy to the waiting world.

A twinkling star shone over the place where the young King lay in Bethlehem. And on the third day of Creation, God had created those *zazillion* stars, which brought The Wise to kneel before him. In their kneeling, with opened treasure chests, they witnessed how Jesus was born a baby and The Sovereign One, and they provided his poor earthly parents with enough to make the necessary trip into Egypt for his well being. *Epiphany* is the third season, where the world continues to search for various sightings of the Christ. The stars shine and twinkle. The world waits to see the Christ sparkle within each of us.

In the spring, farmers begin to cultivate the ground and make it ready to receive new seed and grain by their reading of the new moon. For on the fourth day of Creation, God created two lights. One was the sun for daylight. The other was the moon to provide light in the night. The period of not seeing was over. There was sufficient light for vision.

The fourth season of The Christian Year is *Lent*, when we are called to pause and take an inner look at ourselves. There is much "light" to see the places we need to have cleansed, be changed, transformed, and made new. Lent is the season when we walk with Jesus to the Cross, and it's his light that allows us to know the way to walk the journey.

On the fifth day of Creation, God called forth creatures to inhabit both land and waters. Living beings, flying birds, and animals of every sort began to run, jump, creep, crawl and make their way through the new universe. God did not let them go off without a blessing. God provided their welfare and their perpetuation by charging them to multiply. And so they did.

Easter is the fifth season of The Christian Year. The Resurrection is a call to new life, new hope, and new blessings for now and throughout eternity. It was at Easter that Jesus Christ rose from the dead and went to hell in order to bring out those who had died earlier and were waiting for release. The multiplication of The Church began with The Grateful Dead, who lived again and walked the streets of Jerusalem! The increase continues.

Pentecost is the sixth season. It is the time when the birthday of The Church of Jesus Christ is celebrated. It is the day when the Holy Spirit came with the breath of fresh wind, tongues of fire, kisses of loving empowerment, and a personal commandment to take the Good News of Jesus Christ and his message to the streets! The scared and intimidated Church had waited, hidden in the upper room. The Holy Spirit came only after their time of introspection and prayer. The individuals who went into that place came out a community of faith-filled folks.

There was a party going on. There was a revolution taking place. Those who had been hiding were no longer afraid, but bold. Those who had denied Jesus were in the public square, exclaiming his Messiah-ship. Those who had been underground came out of the closet! For it was the day of new creatures in Christ. Just like the sixth day of God's creation, when the human ones were formed of the dust of the earth and breathed into with the breath of life, it happened again! "It was good." No! "It was very good!"

On the seventh day of Creation, God rested. Our seventh and final season is called Ordinary Time. It is the time when we, The Church, are called to be faithful to the mission and ministry of Jesus Christ without the fanfare of festivals and celebrations. It's a journey of growth in faithfulness, discipleship, and stewardship. During this period, the color is green. And it is the longest season of The Church Year. Like God, we rest from Trinity Sunday until Christ The King Sunday at the end of the season, just before Advent calls us again.

The Christian Year helps us to rehearse God's Story over and over again. It helps us to remember The Creation of the world, which was a "birthday gift" to every human inhabitant. In the beginning of time, God had to push back eternity and create time for us. It's an awesome story. It needs to be known. And it needs to be told, again and again. The Story of God is The Church's story. The Story of God is that of the People who lived before us and left us a world to leave others. The Story of God is a teaching tale which provides much information every time we hear it, rehearse it, and tell it to those who have never heard.

Around the fourth century, The Christian Year became an accepted practice in The Church. New Converts were taken through it for an entire year before Baptism and The Lord's Supper on that following Easter Sunday. The Christian Year is a method of indoctrinating new disciples. The Christian Year is a way of making sense out of the compilation of those 66 books of history we now call the Holy Bible.

All books need an " In the beginning"! The Creation story is only one way of trying to help us make sense of The Christian Year. It looks at God's Story systematically and gives us hopes, promises, warnings, and admonitions as we journey. The Christian Year provides us with great sections of God's Story, which many of the faithful never read at home due to the strange words, violence, and mayhem involved. But it's all part of God's Story. It should be read in The Church. It needs to be taught in the Church. And it needs to be understood by those who call themselves followers of The Way of Christ.

A Word About The Revised Common Lectionary

The Revised Common Lectionary was created in 1992 so that there would be a collection of readings from scriptures that could be read in Churches across the world each Sunday, thereby connecting Christians, regardless of denominations. Since the early fourth century, there have been special days, seasons, and festivals that used the same passages or lections. It is from this source that the Common Lectionary made its way from the Catholic Church to other mainline denominations. Use of a Lectionary is not a "standard" pattern in most Black congregations, although many denominations provide them as part of their Christian Year.

The "appeal" of a Lectionary is that it allows congregations to hear parts of the Bible that they would not read on their own. The Holy Scriptures were intended to be read aloud to audiences. Reading in the worship service is a great aid, a necessary consolation, and a method of getting congregations to move past their favorite passages, which make up their personal "canon" of scripture. If your congregation is one that does not make use of a regular calendar of passages to be read during the worship service, there are several ways that other scriptures might be included. The deacons, who begin many worships, could be asked to help the choir by using the passage that the Anthem will uplift. A member of the choir could read a particular passage just before the choir sings to provide the context for the words and music that will follow.

There are multitudes of needs that sit in our pews, and what has led us to preach and sing does not necessarily touch all the hurts, pains, and wounds. However, when we make it a habit to read an Old Testament lesson followed by the Psalm, it can work its healing mystery without the follow-up sermon of explanation. People need to know that the God of "old" is alive, well, and operating in our "today"! The Lectionary ties the Old Testament "testimony" to the Psalm for us. The Old Testament passage should be read first. Then the Lectionary provides for us the "thoughts of reflection" through the Psalms that the later Church remembered and rehearsed about the "former" acts of God on the nation's behalf. We are those who now need to hear the "old" stories and to remember that God continues to act on our behalf!

Another "appeal" of the Lectionary is that it allows continuous portions of scripture to be heard, read, and expounded upon over a course of three years. Year A of The Revised Common Lectionary focuses on the book of Matthew. It also provides for us the stories of the Patriarchs, Matriarchs, and Moses the Law Giver. Year B uses the book of Mark as its Gospel. King David and the historical books are its focus. John is used around Christmas and Easter in Year B. Year C takes us through the book of Luke and tells the ministry of both Elijah and Elisha. During the Easter Season, we are taken through the Acts of The Apostles, which replaces the Old Testament lessons. Psalms are used throughout all three years to give reflection upon the Hebrew scripture and should be read in this manner.

As a preacher of color, this "rigid" structure didn't "sit" well with me when I first heard of it in seminary. I fought it, because I felt that it didn't allow me freedom in The Holy Spirit. But I forced myself to try it. I pushed myself to see whether or not God "could" speak to me. And I came to discover that my life was made richer, fuller, and more inclusive by its use. It pushed me to "hear" God speak to me! It was out of my spiritual growth that I begin to preach, to call congregations to worship, and to work with musicians to bless those in the pew.

With four scriptures each week to read, digest, and study, there was more than I could possibly use on a Sunday morning. Therefore, our Bible Studies and Sunday Schools were enriched. And I could do sermon prep with pastors in my area who were using the same scriptures. It became a necessary tool for me to "see" what God had to say to me about me!

Therefore, I offer this "gift" to you as a spiritual growth aid. Try it. You'll like it!

A Word about the Musical Selections

Martin Luther once said that music is a gift of God "instilled and implanted in all creatures...from the beginning of the world. Nothing is without sound or harmony, but the human voice is the most wonderful gift of all. Therefore, next to the Word of God, music deserves the highest praise."

It is in that spirit that I have had the distinct privilege of entering into a harmonious partnership with Reverend Dr. Linda H. Hollies to make this project possible. Dr. Hollies has provided the Scripture lessons, focus, prayers, and visual arts suggestions for each Sunday from Advent through Pentecost. My task has been to provide musical suggestions that will complement, enhance, reinforce, and support the texts and focus of the day.

While my musical suggestions are not intended to be the complete, final, or definitive selections, they are offered to provide a general direction and focus for planning music for the worship service for the various Sundays. The possibilities are endless! Composers are always writing new compositions, and previously written compositions are being uncovered and reprinted.

Because no particular hymnal in the African American church could provide all of the variety and diversity needed for the scope of this project, I have selected the following hymnals for consideration along with their abbreviations throughout this book:

AAHH   *African American Heritage Hymnal* (Chicago: GIA Publications, 2001)

AME   *AMEC Bicentennial Hymnal* (Nashville: The African Methodist Episcopal Church, 1984)

AMEZ   *The African Methodist Episcopal Zion Bicentennial Hymnal* (New York: The African Methodist Episcopal Zion Church, 1996)

LEVS   *Lift Every Voice and Sing II: An African American Hymnal* (New York: The Church Hymnal Corporation, 1993)

LMGM   *Lead Me, Guide Me: The African American Catholic Hymnal* (Chicago: GIA Publications, 1987)

YL   *Yes, Lord! Church of God in Christ Hymnal* (Memphis: The Church of God In Christ Publishing Board, 1982)

HG   *Hymns for the Gospels* (Chicago: GIA Publications, 2001)

Other resources for spirituals and organ music that I frequently recommend include the following:

The Oxford Book of Spirituals. Edited by Moses Hogan (New York: Oxford University Press, 2002)

The Anthology of African American Organ Music, Volumes 1-4. Edited by Dr. Mickey Thomas Terry (St. Louis, MO; Morning Star Music Publishers) [ongoing]

Songs of Deliverance: Organ Arrangements and Congregational Acts of Worship for the Church Year Based on African American Spirituals. By William Farley Smith (Nashville: Abingdon Press, 1996)

After considering the scripture lessons and focus for the Sunday, specific themes, emphases, and key words emerged that guided my selection of appropriate hymns, anthems, spirituals, and gospel selections, as well as organ music. I am certainly aware of the various levels of ability and competency among church music personnel and the variety of instruments that exist in African American churches, and have offered a variety of selections that I hope will provide direction for your thinking and selection process.

Noticeably absent from the listings are suggestions for children's choirs, handbells, instrumental ensembles, and praise and worship teams. It is my hope that titles listed will provide adequate ideas and insight for making those selections. I do not claim to be a specialist in those areas, and therefore make no attempt to offer suggestions. However, a project that includes those selections is much needed.

Pastors, music directors, musicians, and worship leaders should invest in a variety of hymnals for their library for a broader use and selection of hymnody for the congregation. The Hymn Society in the United States and Canada provides the most current and reliable resources for church music. I strongly recommend membership in that organization. The toll free number is 1(800) THE HYMN.

While the accessibility of musical resources written by African Americans has been rather limited in the past, there are more musical selections available now than ever. Most of today's current gospel music by recording artists is available in sheet music and can be ordered from local music dealers. I have personally experienced a tremendous amount of cooperation and success with "N" Time Music in Charlotte, NC. They offer gospel sheet music, songbooks, cassettes and CDs, performance soundtracks and much more. Their address is 4913 Albermarie Road, Suite 103, Charlotte, NC 28205. Their email address is info@ntimemusic.com, and the website is www.ntimemusic.com.

I have also enjoyed many years of reliable, dependable, and courteous service with Lois Fyfe Music in Nashville, TN for all of my choral music and organ music needs. Their address is 2814 Blair Blvd, Nashville, TN 37212. They can also be reached by calling toll free 1(800) 851-9023. Every choir director and musician should establish a consistent and amicable relationship with a music dealer, which brings me to a very critical issue.

I am most obligated to share with the reader that it is illegal to photocopy music! Composers of great music can not and will not benefit from our illegal photocopying and reproduction of their music. The rewards for their work that we so enjoy are never experienced as long as good, God-fearing church choir directors and musicians keep running to the photocopier and illegally reproducing their music. There are very stringent laws that protect these composers, and it is the responsibility of the church Leaders to insure that those laws are not violated. Please be very mindful of this as you select and perform music.

I am indebted to my friend and colleague, Tony McNeill, Director of Music Ministries at the Friendship Missionary Baptist Church in Charlotte, NC, for allowing me to include his research in the Appendix, which contains descriptions of extended sacred works by contemporary African American composers. The Selected Bibliography is intended to recommend additional resources that will provide assistance in planning music for worship.

In his classic book, *Church Music and Theology*, Eric Routley said, "When the minister and musician refuse to communicate with one another...at worst it will be, as it often in practice is, a wicked waste of an opportunity for glorifying God through fruitful partnership." It is my sincere hope and prayer that *Waiting to Go!* will provide an ongoing opportunity for dialogue and communication between the minister and the musician. This "fruitful partnership," so desperately needed, will provide a wonderful catalyst by which the pulpit and the choir loft can more effectively lead the People of God in worship. This kind of planning and collaboration will certainly elevate and enhance music and worship in the African American church to new and ultimate dimensions that please and honor God!

—James Abbington

Christ the King Sunday and Thanksgiving

Christ The King Sunday

Appropriate Banner and Altar Colors: Gold or White
Year A: Ezekiel 43: 11-16, 20-24, Psalm 100, Ephesians 1: 15-23, Matthew 25: 31-46
Year B: 2 Samuel 23: 1-7, Psalm 132: 1-12, Revelation 1: 4b-8, John 18: 33-37
Year C: Jeremiah 23: 1-6, Luke 23: 33-43, Colossians 1: 11-20, Luke 23: 33-43

CALL TO WORSHIP

Leader: O, Come let us adore him!

People: Friend, you have gotten ahead of yourself. It is not Christmas yet.

Leader: O, Come let us adore him!

People: Have you gotten stuck? Why are you repeating yourself?

Leader: O, Come let us adore him!

People: O, Come let us adore him for he is Christ The King!
We come to offer our thanks and our praise.

FOCUS

The Good Shepherd who loves the sheep, cares for the sheep, and protects the sheep from any danger or harm is the prevailing metaphor for this worship experience. Christ is King to the glory of God. The Christ did not look like a king. The Christ did not come to earth as a king. The Christ had no political or military ambitions. But The Christ slipped into human skin, was carried in a virgins womb, was born in a lowly stable, and laid in a manger with swaddling cloths. What a deceiving looking Savior! This One who declares that in The Judgement many of us will be lost due to looking at the wrong People as "select" for God's Realm and overlooking others. Could Christ the King be hidden in the poor, the hungry, the least, the last, and the lost? Where do we seek Christ The King? Could we have missed Christ The King?

VISUAL ARTS

A shepherd's staff is a great visual aid for the altar, along with a crown that symbolizes The Royal Diadem. Rich, royal purple Kente Cloth is another reminder of the divinity of Jesus Christ, which drapes an altar well. The overhead pictures might rotate between that of a crown, a staff, and People being served food, clothing, housing, and educational ministries of many sorts.

Musical Suggestions for Christ the King Sunday

Hymns for the Day

Title	AAHH	AME	AMEZ	LEVS	LMGM	YL	HG
A Child of the King	125	298	542	•	•	118	•
All Hail the Power (CORONATION)	292	4	32	•	88	10	•
All Hail the Power (DIADEM)	293	5	33	•	89	•	•
All Hail the Power (MILES LANE)	294	6	34	•	•	•	•
Crown Him with Many Crowns	288	174	199	•	68	•	•
Jesus Is Our King	•	•	•	•	91	•	•
Jesus Shall Reign	289	96	390	•	•	•	•
Majesty	171	•	246	•	•	•	•
O Worship the King	•	12	4	•	•	3	•
Rejoice, the Lord Is King	•	88	197	•	93	13	•
He Is King of Kings (RIDE ON)	•	•	•	96	•	235	•
Ride On, Jesus, Ride (Gospel)	•	•	•	97	264	•	•
Ride On, King Jesus	255	•	•	•	•	•	•

Anthems

Last Words of David *Randall Thompson*
My Eternal King *Jane Marshall*
All Hail the Power (MILES LANE)
  Ralph Vaughan Williams
O Worship the King *arr. Wendell C. Woods*
All Hail the Power of Jesus' Name *arr. John F. Wilson*

Spirituals

Ride On, King Jesus *Moses Hogan*
Ride On, King Jesus *arr. Howard A. Roberts*
He Is King of Kings #235 YL
Ain't Got Time to Die *Hall Johnson*

Gospel Selections

Ride On, King Jesus #225 AAHH
Sovereign *Carol Antrom*

Organ Music

Partita on Darwall's 148th *Charles Callahan*
Crown Him with Many Crowns *Michael Burkhart*
For He Is King of Kings! *arr. William Farley Smith* (from *Songs of Deliverance*)

THANKSGIVING

Appropriate Banner and Altar Colors: Red or White
Year A: Deuteronomy 8: 7-18, Psalm 65, 2 Corinthians 9: 6-15, Luke 17: 11-19
Year B: Joel 2: 21-27, Psalm 126, 1 Timothy 2: 1-7, Matthew 6:25-33
Year C: Deuteronomy 26: 1-11, Psalm 100, Philippians 4: 4-9, John 6: 25-35

CALL TO WORSHIP

Oh, give thanks unto the Lord who is worthy of laud, honor, and praise! We come to worship the Creator, The Sustainer, and the Omnipotent One who gives water to the earth, trees and seed for grain, knows the snowflakes by name, made animals for reproduction, and prepares an annual harvest for us year after year. It is a good thing to pause and observe the lavish beneficence of The Almighty, who grants us the ability to be recipients again of the ingathering of new and fresh crops. What a mighty God we serve, who with simple care provides for every creature, from the least to the greatest! The angels bow before The God of Heaven, who created the earth and in adoration cares for each and everyone! What a mighty God we serve who connects us all in the web of life. We will stand in adoration of this, our God, who was gracious enough to send us the gift of The Only Begotten Son. It's time to praise The Lord!

(Praise Dancers enter as choir sings *What A Mighty God We Serve!*)

FOCUS

Although Thanksgiving is not an "official" part of the Christian Year but a national day of celebration, we are obligated to include it in our Lectionary considerations. This is another prime opportunity to assist congregations with looking forward to The Coming Christ event. By God's mercies, the people who were no people, had no land, and no political clout, were led from bondage into freedom and fed by the Mighty Hand of God with the food of angels. The manna of the wilderness is seen in The One who came as the Bread of Life. In order to be thankful, one is forced to remember, to recall, and to reflect. Aretha Franklin sang the song, *You'd Better Think*! This festive celebration mandates that we "think" of God's goodness to us day by day. For the reality is that every day for Christians is Thanksgiving!

VISUAL ARTS

Cornucopia is filled with fruit, vegetables, and fresh flowers. It is surrounded by fresh, flowing waterfalls, and even bushel baskets of dirt. The smell of fresh baking breads helps us to think of the fact that The Bread of Life is the reason for our gathering and not the simple call of a national holiday. An overhead with photos of mixed generations at prayer around tables helps us to focus on those who may be forced to eat their bread alone on this day of feasting.

Musical Suggestions For Thanksgiving

Hymns for the Day

Title	AAHH	AME	AMEZ	LEVS	LMGM	YL	HG
Come, Ye Thankful People, Come	194	574	243	•	205	•	•
Count Your Blessings	533	•	626	•	•	35	•
For All the Blessings of the Year	•	577	116	•	•	•	•
For the Beauty of the Earth	•	578	6	•	•	68	•
Now Thank We All Our God	•	573	22	•	208	•	•
We Gather Together	342	576	28	•	307	8	•

Gospel Selections	AAHH	AME	AMEZ	LEVS	LMGM	YL	HG
I Am So Grateful	•	•	•	•	207	•	•
I Thank You, Jesus	532	•	•	•	•	•	•
I Will Bless Thee, O Lord	530	•	•	•	•	•	•
One More Day	538	•	•	•	•	•	•

Anthems

I Will Give Thanks Unto Thee, O Lord *G. Rossini*
Give Thanks to the Lord *Willis L. Barnett*
O Give Thanks Unto the Lord (No. 33 in *Yes, Lord!*)
  Iris Stevenson
Lord, We Give Thanks Unto Thee *Undine Smith Moore*
It Is a Good Thing to Give Thanks *David Hurd*

Spirituals

I Want to Thank You, Lord *Moses Hogan/arr. Benjamin Harlan*

Gospel Selections

For Every Mountain *Kurt Carr*

Organ Music

Now Thank We All Our God *Sigfried Karg-Elert*
Psalm of Praise (Toccata on OLD HUNDREDTH) *Charles Callahan*
We Thank Thee, God (Sinfonia to *Cantata No. 29*) *J. S. Bach/arr. Robert Hebble*
Festive Processional on Now Thank We All Our God *Michael Burkhardt*
Thanksgiving Suite *Charles Callahan*
Postlude on "Old Hundreth" *Fred Bock*

ADVENT

Advent 1

Appropriate Banner and Altar Colors: Purple or Blue
Year A: Isaiah 2: 1-5/ Psalm 122/ Romans 13: 11-14/Matthew 24: 36-44
Year B: Isaiah 64: 1-9/ Psalm 80: 1-19/1Corinthians 1: 2-9/ Mark 13: 24-37
Year C: Jeremiah 33: 14-16/Psalm 25: 1-10/1 Thessalonians 3: 9-13/Luke 21: 25-36

Focus

The first Sunday in Advent is a time to remind the people of God that Christ has come and that Christ will come again! Every scripture is a clarion call to awake from our lethargy and prepare for the return of Jesus Christ, who will be seeking a Church without spot or wrinkle! The scriptures are all aimed at showing the Hebrew "wait" for the Messiah and the fulfillment of Jesus as the Savior. They are filled with both eschatological and apocalyptic language, which heralds the end of time as we know it currently.

It is imperative that we stress the emphasis of a sure return! Prophecy was fulfilled. Prophecy is being fulfilled. And prophecy will be fulfilled. We are in the stage of preparing. Dr. Samuel Dewitt Proctor challenged us with a sermon that asked, "What Have You Done With His First Coming?" It's a worthy message to consider.

On the flip side of our waiting for Jesus Christ to show up is the waiting God does on us! What is God waiting on "us" to do so that the Second Coming might yield a mighty, victorious harvest of souls? There is waiting on both sides of the heavens! This too is a worthy message to consider.

Prayer for Candle Lighting

God, we are now in a posture of waiting. We are your people and waiting has been our constant theme. Our hearts grow weary during our multiple waits. It seems, at times, as if we have been forgotten. And often we attempt to fight for our own freedom with human methods. But Advent has come. Advent reminds us that the wait is almost over. In eager anticipation, we light this candle. It is a symbol of our expectant spirits. It reminds us that you are waiting on us to fulfil our divine destiny! We pray that your wait is fruitful throughout our lives. For it is in the name of The God who comes that we pray. Amen.

Visual Arts

The Hanging of the Greens and sanctuary decorations may be done prior to this first Sunday. If an overhead is used, a photo of a racer at the starting line is a signal that we are on a serious journey and it's time to go! Clocks are additional symbols to be considered. On this day, it is appropriate to place an empty manger in the middle of the altar, anticipating the Holy Family who is coming.

Musical Suggestions for Advent 1

Hymns for the Day

Title	AAHH	AME	AMEZ	LEVS	LMGM	YL	HG
Come, Thou Long-Expected Jesus	•	103	90	•	•	•	•
Emmanuel, Emmanuel	189	•	•	•	•	•	•
O Come, O Come Emmanuel	188	102	92	•	3	•	•
While We Are Waiting, Come	190	•	•	•	•	•	•

Gospel Selections	AAHH	AME	AMEZ	LEVS	LMGM	YL	HG
Soon and Very Soon	193	•	•	14	4	•	•
Christ Is Coming	•	•	•	6	10	•	•
Prepare Ye the Way of the Lord	•	•	•	11	2	•	•

Anthems

Lo, How a Rose E'er Blooming #106 AMEZ

And the Glory of the Lord (from "Messiah"
 G. F. Handel

Every Valley *John Ness Beck*

E'en So Lord Jesus Quickly Come *Paul Manz*

Anthem for Advent *David Davenport, text/
 arr. Eugene Butler*

Spirituals

I Wanna Be Ready *James Miller*

I Want to Be Ready *arr. Roy L. Belfield, Jr.*

Organ Music

Toccata on 'Veni Emmanuel' *Adolphus Hailstork*

Sleepers Wake! A Voice Is Calling, BWV 645 *J. S. Bach*

Behold, a Rose Breaks Into Bloom, Op. 122, No. 8 *Johannes Brahms*

6 Advent Improvisations *Paul Manz*

ADVENT 2

Appropriate Banner and Altar Colors: Blue or Purple
Year A: Isaiah 11: 1-10, Psalm 72:1-7, 18-19, Romans 15: 4-13, Matthew 3: 1-12
Year B: Isaiah 40: 1-11, Psalm 85: 1-2, 8-13, 2 Peter 3: 8-15, Mark 1: 1-8
Year C: Malachi 3: 1-4, Luke 1: 68-79, Philippians 1: 3-11, Luke 3: 1-6

Focus

The theme running through these passages of scripture call for us to be living in a state of active anticipation and expectation of Jesus Christ cracking the skies any day now! John the Baptist calls out a certain warning to all of those who trek out to the desert for the "new act" of water baptism. As for the runner for Jesus the Christ, we want to hear a nice word, a soothing message, and a consoling voice. But John calls the "good" people snakes! John calls them to clean up their pious talking with the proof of their lives. He asks them the question worthy of repeating in our time: How are you living today? The question is pertinent; for Christ is coming again.

When Christ comes, it is expected that justice and peace will reign. It is anticipated that the people of God will be the prime role models of both the hope and the promise of relieving oppression everywhere. We are to be the fruits of righteousness. We are those who are called to walk our talk so that the world might see Jesus in our lives. By our lives, we call out John's warning that, "God is coming! Get it together!" We are the first ones who need to confess, repent, and live godly lives! How do we bring peace into our current worlds of living?

Prayer for Candle Lighting

We are those who are waiting for the new heavens and new earth. We long for the days when violence, misery, and degradation are over, done, finished, and through! We yearn to walk upon The King's Highway and receive our crowns of righteousness! Therefore, we light this candle as a symbol of our expectant spirits. May the candle of expectation light our way, kindle our hopes, and help us be better prepared for the second coming of The Christ.

Visual Arts

The manger that was set out last week might have a twinkling star placed over it. Shepherds and sheep might be added this week, along with other barnyard animals. The congregation can actively participate in this growing and waiting activity with prior announcements.

Musical Suggestions for Advent 2

Hymns for the Day

Title	AAHH	AME	AMEZ	LEVS	LMGM	YL	HG
Behold, Your God	•	•	•	2	•	•	•
On Jordan's Bank	•	•	•	•	8	•	•
On Jordan's Stormy Banks	586	479	550	9	•	165	•
We're Marching to Zion	590	520	•	12	•	24	•

Spirituals	AAHH	AME	AMEZ	LEVS	LMGM	YL	HG
By and By	•	•	•	3	•	•	•
I Wanna Be Ready	600	510	•	7	•	•	•
Jesus Getting Us Ready	•	•	•	•	•	273	•

Gospel Selections	AAHH	AME	AMEZ	LEVS	LMGM	YL	HG
Let Jesus Fix It for You	•	•	•	86	•	307	•
Sign Me Up	192	•	•	142	111	•	•
We Shall Behold Him	583	•	•	•	•	•	•

Anthems

An Advent Processional *David Hurd*
Wait for the Lord *Willis Barnett*
Wake, Awake, for the Night Is Flying
  Jacob Praetorius. arr. John Kingsbury

Carol of the Advent *David Hurd*
The Eyes of All Wait Upon Thee *Jean Berger*

Spirituals

I Want to Be Ready *arr. Ted Hunter*

Come By Here *arr. Uzee Brown*

Gospel Selections

Wait 'til the Morning Comes *V. Michael McKay*

We Shall Behold Him *Dottie Rambo/arr. Larry Mayfield*

Organ Music

Swing Low, Sweet Chariot *Ralph Simpson*
Five Advent Hymn Improvisations *Michael Burkhardt*
Variations on "Kum Ba Yah" *John A. Behnke*
O Zion, When the Bridegroom Comes! *William Farley Smith*

ADVENT 3

Appropriate Banner and Altar Colors: Blue, Purple or Rose
Year A: Isaiah 35: 1-10, Psalm 146: 5-10, James 5: 7-10, Matthew 11: 2-11
Year B: Isaiah 61: 1-4, 8-11, Psalm 126, 1 Thessalonians 5: 16-24, John 1: 6-8, 19-28
Year C: Zephaniah 3: 14-20, Isaiah 12: 2-6, Philippians 4: 4-7, Luke 3: 7-18

Focus

"Are you the one, or should we seek another?" This is a day for good questions. There are many who don't like the business of waiting. Waiting seems too passive. Waiting seems as if there is nothing going on or being accomplished. So many have left The Way seeking other gods. Many have walked off because their questions about who they were waiting on were not sufficiently answered. Questions demand that we spend time setting forth our case for waiting on The One who has come, is here, and will come again.

"Are you the one, or should we seek another?" This is the question that John's disciples ask of Jesus while John is waiting to be beheaded for his faith in his cousin. As a matter of fact, it was John who sent them to Jesus. And Jesus did not give them a simple *yes* or *no* answer. He instead points to the deeds he has already performed. It tells them not to look at him, but to be witnesses to the ways he has already impacted the world around him. What a testimony! How do "they" know that The One we are serving is worth waiting on by the fruit of our life?

The promise we have in our time of waiting is sure: "Those who go out weeping, bearing the seed for sowing, shall come home with shouts of joy, carrying their sheaves," (Psalm 126: 5). So, we wait!

Prayer for Candle Lighting:

God, many have tired of the waiting. Many have turned and walked away. Yet there is a faithful remnant. We have gathered to light this candle of promise. For your promises are sure.

Thank you for the multiple promises you have given us in your Holy Word. And just as the seeds we have planted will sprout in the proper time, after resting, nesting, and growing in the nurture of Mother Earth, we will also bloom as roses in the desert if we wait. On your promises alone, we light this candle of promise. Hear our prayer in the Name of The Promised One who came before and will come again.

Visual Arts

This week is a week for the bringing of the Wise Ones. They should be placed at a distance to indicate their being on the journey. Angels can make an appearance since they have played a part in the messages to all the primary characters, including Zachariah, Elizabeth, Mary, and Joseph. A pregnant woman on a donkey and a man walking alongside the donkey can be an overhead visual.

Musical Suggestions for Advent 3

Hymns for the Day

Title	AAHH	AME	AMEZ	LEVS	LMGM	YL	HG
Are You the Coming One?	•	•	•	•	•	•	71
Hail to the Lord's Anointed (ELLACOMBE)	•	107	109	•	•	•	•
Hail to the Lord's Anointed (SHEFFIELD)	187	•	•	•	•	•	•
Hail to the Lord's Anointed (WESTWOOD)	•	•	110	•	•	•	•
Where Shall I Be?	196	503	•	•	•	•	•

Spirituals	AAHH	AME	AMEZ	LEVS	LMGM	YL	HG
My Lord! What a Morning	195	484	•	13	9	•	•
My Lord! What a Mourning	•	•	609	•	•	•	•

Gospel Selections	AAHH	AME	AMEZ	LEVS	LMGM	YL	HG
Going to Heaven to Meet the King	•	•	•	•	•	160	•
The King Is Coming	•	•	•	•	•	270	•

Anthems

Lift Up Your Heads *John L. Bell*

Lift Up Your Heads Samuel *Coleridge-Taylor*

Advent Carol *Dale Wood*

Inflammatus et Accensus (When Thou Comest) *G. Rossini*

Spirituals

Keep Your Lamps! *arr. Andre Thomas*
 (#19 in *The Oxford Book of Spirituals*)

Would You Be Ready *arr. Uzee Brown, Jr.*

A City Called Heaven *arr. Leonard de Paur*
 (#15 in *The Oxford Book of Spirituals*)

Gospel Selections

Time to Go *John D. Guyton, Jr.*

When the Trumpet Sounds *Andre Thomas*

My Lord Will Come Again *David Haas*

Organ Music

Fantasy and Fugue on 'My Lord, What a Morning' *Ralph Simpson*

Prelude on 'O Fix Me' *J. Roland Braithwaite*

Variations on "Es ist ein' Ros' (Lo, How a Rose E'er Blooming) *Alice Jordan*

Prelude on "Es ist ein' Ros'entsprungen" *Gordon Young*

ADVENT 4

Appropriate Banner and Altar Colors: Purple or Blue
Year A: Isaiah 7: 10-16, Psalm 80: 1-7, 17-19, Romans 1: 1-7, Matthew 1: 18-25
Year B: 2 Samuel 7: 1-11, Luke 1: 47-55, Romans 16: 25-27, Luke 1: 26-38
Year C: Micah 5: 2-5, Luke 1: 47-55, Hebrews 10: 5-10, Luke 1: 39-45

Focus

The Magnificat is a song of praise that cannot be ignored. For centuries, the Church has lifted Mary's song of exaltation after the annunciation by the angel and a visit to her cousin, Elizabeth, who was pregnant with John, The Baptizer. Both of these women have played significant roles in the Christ event. Elizabeth, the barren wife of the priest Zechariah, is pregnant by a mute who would not receive the Word of the Lord! Mary, engaged to Joseph, is a virgin who comes from a peasant background. Joseph seems to have forgotten the story told in Synagogue "a virgin shall bring forth a child." He decides to "put her away, privately." But the angels are working overtime, giving messages, directions, and assurances! Mary is told to go and see her pregnant cousin, and when she is affirmed, her mouth opens as she sings praise to God. Mary is a psalmist! She sings a part of Hannah's prayer. She sings a portion of the Psalms.

She sings a bit of Job's prayer-song. Combining them all, she recognizes that God uses ordinary People; People who are willing to give their all to God's command. Thank God for Dannibelle Hall, who put a contemporary bend to Mary's age-old song. Thank God for a barren woman and a virgin who waited on God! What is the theme song of our life?

Prayer for Candle Lighting

God, you called both Elizabeth and Mary from obscurity and insignificance to the forefront of Your Story! You gave them both leading roles in the drama of salvation's history. They each gave their best to bring Emmanuel, God with us, into the waiting world. On their behalf, we light this candle of hope. It is our hope that our waiting on you will find us faithful and willing to be used when you call. O, come, O come, Emmanuel, in whose name we pray and in whose faith we wait.

Visual Aids

The only article added to the altar today is the manger. The stage is set. We are awaiting the arrival of The God who comes! The overhead picture can be that of children gazing at mangers or of different people watching the star lit sky. Animals in a barn tell the age-old story as well as shepherds watching their flocks at night. The whole world is waiting.

Musical Suggestions for Advent 4

Hymns for the Day

Title	AAHH	AME	AMEZ	LEVS	LMGM	YL	HG
O Come, O Come Emmanuel	188	102	92	•	3	•	•
Waken, O Sleeper	•	•	•	•	•	•	89
When to Mary, the Word	•	•	•	•	•	•	144

Gospel Selections	AAHH	AME	AMEZ	LEVS	LMGM	YL	HG
O Magnify the Lord	•	•	•	•	83	14	•

Anthems

Ave Maria *R. Nathaniel Dett*
Listen to the Lambs *R. Nathaniel Dett*
My Soul Doth Magnify the Lord *Noah Ryder*
Hail Mary *William L. Dawson*
Song of Mary *Harold Friedell*

Spirituals

Mary Had a Baby *arr. William L. Dawson*

Gospel Selections

Mary's Canticle *Leon Roberts*
Behold, the Handmaid of the Lord *Carlton Burgess*

Organ Music

Prelude on "Es ist ein' Ros' ensprugen" *Gordon Young*
5 Advent Hymn Improvisations *Michael Burkhardt*
Prelude on "Let All Mortal Flesh Keep Silence" *Albert L. Travis*
Ave Maria *Franz Schubert / arr. Raymond Herbek*
Magnificat 1-6 *Marcel Dupré* (from *Fifteen Pieces*)

CHRISTMASTIDE

Christmas Season

The Hope of the world is Jesus! We celebrate his moving into our skin, sharing our humanity, and winning for us the victory over death, the grave, and hell. Christmas is not simply one day. Christmas is a season of sharing the mystery of God's love manifested in Jesus Christ. Christmas is a season of wonder, where the Babe in Bethlehem captures the attention of the whole world. Christmas is the season of new hope, new joy, and a newfound sense of community. May this be a Mary's Christmas for you and your congregation! Be alert for angels. Watch for the illuminating stars. Prepare to see him, like the shepherds. Be in tune with the angelic songs. Open your heart and allow there to be room in the inn of your heart!

Christmas is the season that leads us into Epiphany, where we are urged to be on the lookout for signs of Christ's presence in our midst.

Christmas Eve

Appropriate Banner and Altar Colors: White
Year A, B, and C: Isaiah 9: 2-7/ Psalm 96/ Titus 2: 11-15/ Luke 2: 1-20
Year A, B, and C: Alternative Lessons 1: Isaiah 62: 6-12/ Psalm 97/ Titus 3: 4-7/ Luke 2: 1-20
Year A, B, and C: Alternative Lessons 2: Isaiah 52: 7-10/ Psalm 98/ Hebrews 1: 1-12/ John 1: 1-14

Focus

On this night or Christmas morning, we join with the angelic choir in offering praise to the newborn King. The whole earth offers God a brand new song of eternal thanks. A generous God has loved so mightily that His love echoes across the world. The splendor of the heavens radiates in each face. Hope is born anew this night. Angels we have heard! Now, the angels will listen to our glad songs! We are called to sing new songs unto God on this most holy of all nights. The elements are joining in this command to offer new songs of praise. From sea to shining sea, from mountaintop to valley low, there are sounds of great joy being lifted unto God. God is great and working on our behalf right now. We have waited in anticipation for this magnificent event of new birth. We know that God has come and tonight we shout, "Encore God, encore!"

The God who has come is present already, even as we wait. We have brought gifts and we have gathered to celebrate before the beauty of this great God who comes again and again. The sky is shouting out its praise with bright stars. We bring our voices and the sounds of cheering applause. Together we offer extravagant thanks for extravagant love, which came to earth on Christmas Day. The God who came will come again. This is our certain hope and our excellent praise!

Candle Lighting

The house and realm of God stand sure forever. The throne of God is established forever. The people of God are loved forever. In memory of every promise made and kept for The Ancestors, we light this candle of anticipation with eternal joy!

Visual Aids

Tonight we complete the altar scene that has been built over Advent. The earthly parents are put in place. A round loaf of brown bread may be placed in the manger, wrapped in the appearance of a blanket of swaddling cloths, to indicate that the newborn baby was born to be Bread for The World and to die for our salvation!

Musical Suggestions for Christmas Eve

Hymns for the Day

Title	AAHH	AME	AMEZ	LEVS	LMGM	YL	HG
A Stable Lamp Is Lighted	198	•	•	•	•	•	•
Away in a Manger	208	113	86	27	•	216	•
It Came Upon a Midnight Clear	215	108	97	•	23	211	•
O Holy Night	201	121	•	•	•	•	•
O Little Town of Bethlehem	204	109	91	•	25	205	•
Silent Night	211	116	93	26	26	217	•

Spirituals	AAHH	AME	AMEZ	LEVS	LMGM	YL	HG
Mary Borned a Baby	•	•	•	22	•	•	•
Rise Up, Shepherd, and Follow	212	123	•	24	12	212	•
That Boy-Child of Mary	8	•	•	25	•	•	•

Gospel Selections	AAHH	AME	AMEZ	LEVS	LMGM	YL	HG
Rise Up, Shepherd, and Follow	213	•	•	•	•	•	•

Anthems

To Bethlehem *David McKinley Williams*
In Silent Night *Mitchell B. Southall*
There Is A Flower *John Rutter*

Spirituals

New Born *John W. Work, III*
Mary Had a Baby *William L. Dawson*
Glory to the Newborn King *arr. Robert L. Morris* (#24 in *The Oxford Book of Spirituals*, p. 194-200)

Gospel Selections

Mary Had a Baby *arr. Roland Carter*
New Born King *Lena McLin*

Organ Music

Spiritual Lullaby *William B. Cooper* (based on a Christmas spiritual "Baby Bethlehem")
Berceuse Paraphrase *George Baker*
I Wonder as I Wander *David Evan Thomas* (from *Augsburg Organ Library–Christmas*)
Pastorale in F Major, BWV 590 *Johann S. Bach*

CHRISTMAS 1

Appropriate Banner and Altar Colors: White
Year A: Isaiah 63: 7-9/Psalm 148/ Hebrews 2: 10-18/Matthew 2: 13-23
Year B: Isaiah 61: 10-62:3/Psalm 148/Galatians 4: 4-7/Luke 2: 22-40
Year C: 1 Samuel 2: 18-20, 26/ Psalm 148/Colossians 3: 12-17/ Luke 2: 41-52

FOCUS

God's love is steadfast. God's promises are sure. God's people are never forgotten. For God comes in flesh to walk among them to show them the way "home" and to lead them to abundant life. The Old Covenant promises are highlighted. The people who have waited, watched, and longed for the Messiah are assured that God is indeed a promise keeper! The infant is presented. This child, like the young Samuel, is filled with the favor of God, people and empowered by the Holy Spirit. The young man debates with the scholars. For this child did not come into the world to live a long life, but to die. The scriptures hasten his childhood, hide his adolescence, and deny us access to his young adult life. In this Christmas season we get only tiny glimpses of the way that the "Son," who was born a child, was received.

THE CHRIST CANDLE LIGHTING

Faithful God, again you have come. Our waiting for you has been fruitful again. Thank you for your love. Thank you for your long suffering with us. Thank you for coming to see about us, personally. This day, we light this candle because you put on our flesh and came to our community to walk our walk and to share your divinity. We are humbled by your coming.

VISUAL ARTS

Old men and old women smiling at babies gives an indication of Simeon and Anna, who have waited to see God's glory. A family dedicating an infant through baptism with a smiling congregation shows how babies touch each of our lives. A Crown over a Cross is another indication that the King of Heaven and Earth has arrived to suffer in our place!

Musical Suggestions for Christmas 1

Hymns for the Day

Title	AAHH	AME	AMEZ	LEVS	LMGM	YL	HG
Angels We Have Heard on High	206	118	•	•	17	207	•
Hark! The Herald Angels Sing	214	115	85	•	13	208	•
Joy to the World	197	120	96	•	19	210	•
O Come, All Ye Faithful	199	106	95	•	20	203	•
While Shepherds Watched Their Flocks	•	•	99	•	•	209	•

Spirituals	AAHH	AME	AMEZ	LEVS	LMGM	YL	HG
Wonderful Counselor	210	•	•	•	•	•	•

Anthems

For Unto Us a Child Is Born (from "Messiah") *G. F. Handel*

Gloria in Excelsis *W. A. Mozart*

A King Is Born *Brent Pierce*

Spirituals

Roun' de Glory Manger *Willis Laurence James*

Sing, Shout! Tell the Story *William Grant Still*
 (from *Christmas in the Western World*)

See the Little Baby *Donald Swift*

Go, Tell It on the Mountain *arr. Roland M. Carter*
 (#22 in *The Oxford Book of Spirituals*, p. 177-183)

Gospel Selections

Hallelujah to the King *Pamela Davis*

The Angels Sang *Margaret Pleasant Douroux*

Glory to the New Born King *A. Carney*

Organ Music

Rhapsodie sur des Noëls *Eugene Gigout*

Variations on "Adeste Fideles" *Marcel Dupré*

In Dulci Jubilo, BWV 751 *Johann S. Bach*

Once in Royal David's City *David Cherwien* (from *Interpretations, Book V*)

Watch Night

Appropriate Banner and Altar Colors: Kente Cloth
Ecclesiastes 3:1–13/Psalms 8/Matthew 25:31–46/Revelation 21:1–6

Focus

This is a service of African American congregations that began as people anticipated "watching out" the last year of slavery. The service of watching and waiting continues.

Watch night worship is a time for reflection, testimonies, and songs of God's grace. It is the period when we voice our determination for the gift of a year to come. Usually an inter-generational service, both youth and seasoned saints can play an important part. History meets the future. Tradition faces hopes. The God of the years is constant. Jesus is the same yesterday, today, and forever.

Altar Focus

A big clock with the hands on five minutes to midnight sits on an altar covered with red, black, and green Kente cloth. Implements of grinders, hoes, spades, and even an old cotton sack become the visual aids. A quilt draping the altar would be another useful article. Stalks of wheat, bolls of cotton, and even tobacco leaves can be placed in vases as "floral" arrangements.

Time is optional, of course. However, the ideal gathering is around a potluck dinner with games for all ages following. Worship should begin around 10:30 PM. Serving breakfast following worship allows the guns of salute to stop and the revelers to find their way inside!

Call to Worship

Leader: Why do we gather on this night?
People: We gather to remember our enslaved past.
Leader: Why do we gather on this night?
People: We gather to celebrate God's keeping powers.
Leader: Why do we gather on this night?
People: We gather to recall God's mercies in the midst of oppression.
Leader: Why do we gather this night?
People: We gather to celebrate our God who journeys with us, year by year.
   All Thanks be unto the ever faithful and true God.

Songs of Praise

Call to Confession

Leader: The year is almost over. Many of the things we made covenant to do in January have fallen by the wayside. Let us seek forgiveness of our sin.

NOTE: This worship is not an "official" part of The Christian Year! It is a Black Church addition as slaves waited for freedom. The Scriptures are recent suggestions. The worship is taken from A Trumpet For Zion, Year B.

Silent Confession

Words of Assurance

Our sins are removed as far as the east is from the west. This is the promise of God. For our God yearns for authentic relationship with us. This is mighty good news.

Call to Remember

Remember God's goodness during the year. Many are the afflictions of the righteous, but the Lord delivers us from them all. Those with willingness are provided these moments to testify to the ways that God has sent victory our way.

Call to Prayer for the New Year

The year is almost over. Our elders taught us how to bow on our knees before the Almighty. Kneeling conveys our humble attitude before God. Kneeling is a symbol of our grateful hearts before the throne of Grace. Let us prepare now to kneel in prayer as we watch for the New Year. Let us praise God together on our knees.

A Covenant of Declarations

Leader: Happy New Year! Thank God for another opportunity to offer praise and thanksgiving to Maker, Redeemer, and Sustainer. Resolutions often last until after breakfast! But our fore-parents made their declarations of intentions for better Christian service as they were empowered by the Holy Spirit. As you are led, please rise and state your intentions to walk with Jesus in this New Year.

Offertory Invitation

Throughout the year, God has been faithful. Our generous response through our sharing is how we say, "Thanks."

Offertory Praise

Beneficent and Gracious Savior, we cannot pay for one second of the year you have brought us through. Yet, we offer these tokens in humble appreciation that as others watch and wait in the coming years, these doors will be open to receive their grateful hearts. In the name of love we pray.

Benediction

Leader: The old has passed and the New Year has arrived.
People: We have a new beginning.
Leader: The Lord of fresh starts has given us a brand new slate.
People: We leave to write new history with our Amazing God.
Leader: Go in the peace and power of the God who holds yesterday, today, and every tomorrow. Remember, you are blessed signs of God's renewing promises as you go your way rejoicing!
People: Amen.

Holy Name of Jesus Day: January 1

Appropriate Banner and Altar Colors: White

Year A, B, and C: Numbers 6:22–27/Psalm 8/Galatians 4:47/Luke 2:15–21

(See AA Heritage Hymnal for Emancipation Day Litany, P. 53)

Call to Worship

Leader: The Name Above All Names summons us today.

People: We have heard the calling of our names.

Leader: The Name Beyond Words commands an accounting.

People: We have heard the calling of our names.

Leader: The Name Above All Names has given us a new name.

People: We bless the wonderful name of Jesus!

Focus

God has called us and named us "children." Like Jesus, who was named Emmanuel before his birth, we have the obligation to live up to our name. Too often we fail to live up to the name "child of God" or "Christian." For like little children, we sometimes act as if we do not hear our name being called! Yet, we do long to walk worthy of our given name. We are children of God who are adopted into the royal family. We are heirs to salvation and eternal life. This is a day to remember the holy name of Jesus and to re-claim our own. Remembrance and confession restores the worth and value of our name.

Benediction

Leader: The Lord bless you and keep you.

People: The Lord's face shine upon you.

Leader: The Lord be gracious unto you.

People: The countenance of the Lord be lifted upon you.

Leader: May the Lord, our God, grant you great shalom! Amen.

People: Halleluia and amen. (Numbers 6: 22-27)

Visual Arts

Broken shackles, chains, and copies of birth certificates make plain the reality that new names are appropriate. A pregnant woman and man looking at a book of names makes another statement to the worth of new names. In the movie *Roots*, there is an awesome photo of an infant being lifted by his father toward The High God. It is the time of introducing the newly named baby to The Creator.

Musical Suggestions for Watch Night

Hymns for the Day

Title	AAHH	AME	AMEZ	LEVS	LMGM	YL	HG
Another Year in Dawning	•	580	113	•	•	•	•
Great Is Thy Faithfulness	158	84	80	189	242	122	•
Guide Me, O Thou Great Jehovah (CWM RHONDDA)	138	52	82	•	•	•	•
Guide Me, O Thou Great Jehovah (ZION)	140	53	•	•	•	31	•
How Great Thou Art	148	68	47	60	181	39	•
I Know Who Holds Tomorrow	415	446	48	•	187	124	•
O God, Our Help in Ages Past	170	61	81	•	230	15	•
To God Be the Glory	157	21	50	•	•	19	•

Spirituals	AAHH	AME	AMEZ	LEVS	LMGM	YL	HG
I Want Jesus to Walk with Me	563	375	514	70	263	381	•

Gospel Selections	AAHH	AME	AMEZ	LEVS	LMGM	YL	HG
He Has Done Great Things for Me	507	•	•	•	289	•	•
He's Done So Much for Me	511	•	•	•	•	•	•
Order My Steps	333	•	•	•	•	•	•
Precious Lord, Take My Hand	471	393	628	106	162	384	•
The Lord Is Blessing Me Right Now	506	•	•	•	•	•	•
We've Come this Far by Faith	412	•	•	208	225	395	•

Anthems

Psalm 150 *Alberto Randegger*

Great Is Thy Faithfulness *arr. Nathan Carter*

Festival Piece on ST. ANNE *Eugene Butler*

Canticle of Praise *John Ness Beck*

Psalm 150 *Nathan Carter*

Let Mt. Zion Rejoice *J. Herbert*

Psalm 46 *John Ness Beck*

Organ Music

The Old Year Now Has Passed Away, BWV 614 *Johann S. Bach*

Prelude and Fugue in E-flat Major, BWV 552 *Johann S. Bach* (*Clavierübung–Part III*)

I Want Jesus to Walk With Me *Richard Billingham* (from *Seven Reflections on African American Spirituals*)

God of Grace, Op. 14 *Paul Manz* (CWM RHONDDA)

CHRISTMAS 2

Appropriate Banner and Altar Colors: White

Year A, B, and C: Jeremiah 31: 7-14/ Psalm 147: 12-20/Ephesians 1: 3-14/ John 1: 1-18

Focus

Jesus did come; not to help pious, or angelic beings, but to redeem, set free, and uplift the descendants of Abraham, Sarah, and Hagar. Jesus became like us to become for us the sacrificial atonement for our sins. Because he was tested by what he suffered, he is able to help us during our times of test. God has more than blessed us in Christ with every spiritual blessing in the heavenly places. We have been adopted into the royal family. We are joint heirs with Christ. We simply gather to worship the Most High God, who is worthy of our praise for freely giving us great grace in the Beloved. Jesus was in the world and the world did not know him. He came unto his own and they did not receive him. But all who receive him and believe in his name have power to be children of God. This is a time for Leadership installations, rededications, and calls to deeper discipleship as we show evidence of having received this most precious gift of Christmas.

Christ Candle Lighting

In Jesus Christ, we have obtained an inheritance. We have been destined, according to the purpose of him who accomplishes all things and his counsel and will, so that we who have set our hope in Christ might live for the praise of his glory. By grace, we are saved. This is good news for lighting this Christ Candle.

Benediction

Leader: The Word has become flesh and has come to live among us.

People: We are the light of the world.

Leader: The world needs to see and to know the Light.

People: We are the light of the world.

Leader: The Word is flesh and lives in you.

People: We are the light of the world! It is so, now and forever more.

Visual Arts

The altar remains the same with an empty manger to signify that Jesus now resides in the cradles of our hearts.

Musical Suggestions for Christmas 2

Hymns for the Day

Title	AAHH	AME	AMEZ	LEVS	LMGM	YL	HG
Angels, from the Realms of Glory	207	119	98	•	18	214	•
Heaven's Christmas Tree	205	•	•	•	•	•	•
Messiah Now Has Come	203	•	•	•	•	•	•
Once in Royal David's City	•	•	102	•	•	•	•
The First Noel	•	111	123	•	28	204	•

Anthems

Sing for Christ Is Born *William Byrd/arr. Hal Hopson*

Christmas *Arthur Willis*

Love Came Down at Christmas *Leo Sowerby*

Unto Us a Child Is Born *Richard Purvis*

Spirituals

African Noel *arr. Andre Thomas*

Two African Carols *arr. John L. Bell*
1. Good News for Everyone
2. Poor Folk Hear Him Gladly

Behold the Star *William L. Dawson*

Gospel Selections

Sing Hallelujah (to the Newborn King) *V. Michael McKay*

God Became Flesh *Carol Antrom*

I Apologize *V. Michael McKay*

Organ Music

Greensleeves *Richard Purvis*

Arietta *Thomas Kerr* (*Anthology of African American Organ Music,* Vol. 1)

Pastorale *William B. Cooper* (*Anthology of African American Organ Music,* Vol. 2)

Rise Up Shepherds, and Follow *William Farley Smith* (from *Songs of Deliverance*)

EPIPHANY

The Season of Epiphany

The Greco-Roman world gave us the word *epiphany*. Epiphany designated for them the occasion when state officials made public appearances within the provinces. The early Church adopted the term to indicate the manifestations of Christ within the world. During Epiphany, we get different snapshots of the Savior's brilliant glory.

The Greek word *epiphaneia* means to manifest, show forth, or make clear. The bright star of Bethlehem guided the Wise to get a glimpse of the newborn Sovereign. During this season of illumination, many sightings of the Divine will help us view the many faceted aspects of our great Savior and the plan for our salvation.

January 6th is the official Feast of Epiphany. This date signals the arrival of the known world to give honor and treasure to Jesus, and also signifies his baptism by John when the full Trinity is displayed.

The intent of the month of January in general is new beginnings, fresh starts, and the additional opportunities that God supplies for us. Its theme should be the light of justice that Jesus' birth brought into the world. Epiphany sightings of Jesus Christ in our world, like baptismal renewals and the Dr. Martin Luther King, Jr. celebration, are priorities of this month. See the *African American Heritage Hymnal* for Litanies.

Altar Focus

To symbolize light, a large, old-fashioned kerosene lamp can be the altar focus for the first Sunday in January. A menorah, with black, red, and green candles, can be placed between the usual Christ candles. When Epiphany is celebrated on the Sunday nearest January 6th, the altar focus can feature water pitchers of various shapes and sizes, goblets, crystal decanters, and treasure chests. This is another liturgical day of white, and gold stars will enhance the world's "illumination."

On the Sunday that the reaffirmation of baptism is celebrated, a large, clear, crystal bowl filled with water or one of the "heritage" wash basins and pitchers can be featured. Conch shells, dried sponges, and assorted seashells call out, "Take me to the water!". The baptismal font and other symbols of baptism are welcomed. The Sunday nearest January 6th is the opportune day for celebrating baptismal renewal. An overhead with a picture of a body of water will carry many of the congregation back to our Southern traditions for baptizing services. Renewals help us focus on "that day and that hour" when we said a bold "YES!" to Jesus Christ for ourselves.

For Dr. King's celebration, a grapevine wreath may be the altar focus, wrapped in black, red, and green cloth or paper, with large red flowers having yellow centers, to represent our homeland and our continuing struggle for liberty and justice. The altar need not be fully changed weekly, but enhanced for the particular liturgical setting of worship.

Epiphany

Appropriate Banner and Altar Colors: White and Gold

See *African American Heritage Hymnal* for Litany

Years A, B, and C: Isaiah 60:1–6/Psalm 72:1–14/Ephesians 3:1–12/Matthew 2:1–12

Focus

Have you not heard? Did you not know? Christ went to Africa! It's a reality that needs to be spread, told, shouted over, and celebrated. God sent the Light of the World to Africa! The spirit of death was seeking to extinguish the Light. Africa was hospitable and welcomed her son home. God designed a goodly land that provided refuge for the Hope of the World! The angel directed Joseph to take The Child and his mother to Egypt. The world celebrates the Wise Ones who came to pay homage. There is not a Nativity Scene anywhere that does not include at least one woman, Mary, and one Black man! So, we need to remind our congregations that people of color have been "included" by God all the time. We are not "newcomers" to the Christian faith.

Relevant to many in our congregation is the manner that God provided the "public welfare" to care for Jesus and his earthly parents! "The wealth of the wicked is laid up for the righteous," the Bible says. The Wise Men were really Harry Potter-type magicians who were priests in their homelands. By the light of a heavenly star, they were led to come and kneel at the manger of The Newborn King. They brought treasure chests with them. It was their provisions that cared for the Holy Family on their Mecca to Africa! It's always amazing, and it's always mysterious, but our God will make a way!

Visual Arts

(Listed on previous pages throughout this season of Epiphany).

Benediction

Leader: The star is yet shining and people are yet looking for the Light of the World!

People: We leave to point the way.

Leader: The manger is empty, and the angelic choir no longer sings.

People: Christ is at home in our hearts! His song of victory is on our lips.

Leader: The light of Christ will lead you, the love of Christ will enfold you, and the spirit of Christ will live through you, world without end! Amen and amen! (Trumpet for Zion, B)

Musical Suggestions for Epiphany

Hymns for the Day

Title	AAHH	AME	AMEZ	LEVS	LMGM	YL	HG
As With Gladness Men of Old	•	124	125	•	•	•	•
Brightest and Best	219	•	126	•	•	•	•
Go, Tell It on the Mountain	202	122	101	21	22	215	•
Jesus, the Light of the World	217	112	111	•	•	•	•
Light of the World, We Hail Thee	•	•	254	•	•	•	•
We Three Kings	218	•	124	•	27	213	•
What Child Is This?	220	•	105	•	29	206	•

Spirituals	AAHH	AME	AMEZ	LEVS	LMGM	YL	HG
Behold the Star	216	•	•	•	•	•	•

Gospel Selections	AAHH	AME	AMEZ	LEVS	LMGM	YL	HG
Shine on Me	527	•	•	•	160	•	•
The Lord Is My Light (P. Mills)	•	•	•	•	•	66	•
The Lord Is My Light	160	•	•	58	132	•	•

Anthems

Awake, Awake *David Hurd*
We Have Seen His Star *David Hurd*
Heavenly Light *A. Kopylov*
Jesu, Bright and Morning *Leo Sowerby*
Brightest and Best *Mark Schweizer*
Adoration of the Wise Men *arr. Crawford R. Thoburn*

Spirituals

Rise, Shine, For the Light is a Comin'
  arr. Roland M. Carter
Behold the Star *William L. Dawson*

Organ Music

Three for Epiphany *Paul Manz*
  1. We Three Kings
  2. As With Gladness Men of Old
  3. O Morningstar, How Fair and Bright
O Morning Star, Christ Jesus *Gerhard Krapf* (from *Third Organ Sonata on Morning Chorales*)
O Morning Star, How Fair and Bright *Max Drischer*
O Morning Star, How Fair and Bright *Paul Manz* (from *Augsburg Organ Library–Epiphany*)

EPIPHANY 1

Appropriate Banner and Altar Colors: Green and White
Year A: Isaiah 42: 1-9/ Psalm 29/Acts 10: 34-43/Matthew 3: 13-17
Year B: Genesis 1: 1-5/Psalm 29? Acts 19: 1-7/Mark 1: 4-11
Year C: Isaiah 43: 1-7/Psalm 29/Acts 8: 14-17/Luke 3: 15-22

Focus

God has a love affair with water! It is no secret that three quarters of the world is water. Three fourths of our bodies is water, and embryonic waters are required for our birth. The symbol of water speaks to life. In the Exodus, the waters parted for new life after deliverance. In the wilderness, the Rock gave up water for survival. At an old well, Jesus spoke to a shame-based sister about giving her living waters as she sought for satisfaction from the many pains she suffered of rejection and abandonment. As Jesus prepares for full time ministry, he goes to the waters because this is another "In the beginning!" God is about to do something new. History is getting ready to be made. So, God and The Holy Spirit show up as Jesus emerges from the waters of baptism. The voice of God is heard saying, "This is my Beloved Child in whom I am well pleased!"

Baptism is a family affair. We don't do "house" baptisms or private ones. We baptize believers in the congregation of believers; for it is a sign that they are joining the worldwide family of God. They have found their way "home" to a local congregation, but their baptism includes them in the family everywhere. What we do after our baptism calls The Voice to speak up on our behalf. We are God's Beloved. The search continues as God seeks those who truly desire to represent in the world.

Perhaps this is the Sunday your local congregation will celebrate the life and ministry of Dr. Martin Luther King, Jr. The holy scriptures help us explain just how the waters of his baptism made him a passionate warrior for justice in the world. The time of trying to "resurrect" Dr. King's dead bones is over! Now is the time we should be challenging congregations about whether or not their baptism has given them passion to perform. Let's allow Dr. King to rest in peace! We need to remember him with love. We need to celebrate his ministry by being active on the course he chartered before his death. He has heard The Voice! What do we hear?

Visual Arts

(On pages prior)

Litanies

See African American Heritage Hymnal

Musical Suggestions for Epiphany 1 (Baptism of the Lord)

Hymns for the Day

Title	AAHH	AME	AMEZ	LEVS	LMGM	YL	HG
Behold, A Sower From A-Far	•	•	356	•	•	•	•
Come, Holy Spirit, Dove Divine	677	•	•	•	•	•	•
Grace Greater Than Our Sin	•	•	343	•	•	132	•
I Have Decided to Follow Jesus	400	•	•	136	118	484	•
Take My Life and Let It Be	•	292	470	•	•	337	•
Wash, O God, Our Sons and Daughters	674	•	•	•	•	•	•

Spirituals	AAHH	AME	AMEZ	LEVS	LMGM	YL	HG
Certainly, Lord	678	•	•	132	121	•	•
Fix Me, Jesus	436	•	•	125	314	•	•
Take Me to the Water	675	•	•	134	108	349	•
Wade in the Water	676	•	602	143	107	114	•

Gospel Selections	AAHH	AME	AMEZ	LEVS	LMGM	YL	HG
He Brought Me Out	509	•	•	•	•	432	•
He Calmed the Ocean	223	•	•	•	•	•	•
Peace! Be Still	221	462	•	•	•	373	•
Shine On Me	527	•	•	•	•	•	•
Your Grace and Mercy	270	•	•	•	•	•	•

Anthems

Father in Heaven *David Hurd*   Let This Mind Be in You *Lee Hoiby*

Spirituals

Wade in the Water *arr. Moses Hogan*   Wade in the Water *arr. Jester Hairston*
Wade in de Water *arr. Harry T. Burleigh*

Organ Music

Wade in du Water *William Farley Smith* (from *Songs of Deliverance*)

All Who Believe and Are Baptized *Richard Proulx* (from *Augsburg Organ Library–Epiphany*)

On Jordan's Bank the Baptist's Cry *Bruce Neswick* (from *Augsburg Organ Library–Epiphany*)

Epiphany 2

Appropriate Banner and Altar Colors: Green
Year A: Isaiah 49: 1-7/ Psalm 40:1-11/ 1 Corinthians 1: 1-9/ John 1: 29-42
Year B: 1 Samuel 3: 1-20/Psalm 139: 1-18/ 1 Corinthians 6: 12-20/John 1: 43-51
Year C: Isaiah 62: 1-5/ Psalm 36: 5-10/ 1 Corinthians 12: 1-11/ John 2: 1-11

Focus

The Light is calling out to the world, "Follow me." The Lamb of God, who takes away the sins of the world, is out seeking those who will become disciples of the way, which is the method and the mission of Christian service to the world. The ministry of Jesus was a mission of reaching the lost, feeding the hungry, healing the sick, raising the dead, and freeing those who were bound. It's only a few weeks since the "babe" was born, but he's on a journey to Calvary and has no time for fooling around. His first miracle is that of attending a community festival, a wedding, and listening to his mother tell the host, who has run out of wine, "Whatever he says, do it." For she has been watching his light. Now others are called to see it.

If this is Dr. Martin Luther King, Jr. celebration Sunday at your local congregation, the boy Samuel becomes an excellent role model for sermon use. Key sentences to ponder saying: "The word of the Lord was rare in those days; visions were not widespread. At that time Eli, whose eyesight had begun to grow dim, was lying down in his room; the lamp of God had not yet gone out.." (1 Samuel 3: 1-3) Is not this the day in which we live? The horror of September 11th calls us to "see" how badly prayer is needed in our nation, in our schools, and in our seats of government. Where are the "visions" of God that bring about justice, peace, and deliverance for people of color across the world? What child might be the "very one" to be "called" by God for service like Dr. Martin Luther King, Jr.? Samuel, and Jesus, were vessels for God in their childhood. How do we include our children in following The Light?

Visual Arts

(See prior altar settings on previous pages)

Benediction

Leader: Leave to be The Church everywhere you go!
People: We leave remembering that all things are lawful but not beneficial.
Leader: Leave to let the world see Jesus shining through your life!
People: We leave knowing that we have been called to be sent to bring others.

(Trumpet For Zion, B)

Musical Suggestions for Epiphany 2

Hymns for the Day

Title	AAHH	AME	AMEZ	LEVS	LMGM	YL	HG
Follow Jesus	356	•	•	•	•	•	•
Footsteps of Jesus	•	•	627	•	•	407	•
Guide Me O Thou Great Jehovah (CMW RHONDDA)	138	52	82	•	•	•	•
Guide Me O Thou Great Jehovah (ZION)	140	53	681	•	•	•	•
Tell Me the Stories of Jesus	•	550	270	•	•	219	•
Where He Leads Me	550	•	•	144	•	409	•

Spirituals	AAHH	AME	AMEZ	LEVS	LMGM	YL	HG
Certainly, Lord	678	•	•	132	121	•	•
Fix Me, Jesus	436	•	•	125	314	•	•
Take Me to the Water	675	•	•	134	108	349	•
Wade in the Water	676	•	602	143	107	114	•

Gospel Selections	AAHH	AME	AMEZ	LEVS	LMGM	YL	HG
A Follower of Christ	•	•	•	•	117	•	•
I've Decided to Make Jesus My Choice	•	•	•	•	112	329	•
Lead Me, Guide Me	474	378	•	194	168	•	•
Precious Lord, Take My Hand	471	393	628	106	162	384	•

Anthems

Jesu, Joy of Man's Desiring *J.S. Bach*   I Waited for the Lord *Felix Mendelssohn*

Spirituals

I Believe This is Jesus *Undine Smith Moore*   Hol' de Light *Hall Johnson*

Gospel Selections

Follow Jesus *Margaret Douroux*   Purpose in Your Heart *Carol Antrom*

Organ Music

God of Grace, Op. 14 *Paul Manz*

Lil' Boy, How Old Are You *William Farley Smith* (from *Songs of Deliverance*)

O God, Our Faithful God, Op. 122, No. 7 *Johann S. Brahms*

Epiphany 3

Appropriate Banner and Altar Colors: Green
Year A: Isaiah 9: 1-4/ Psalm 27: 1-9/1 Corinthians 1: 10-18/ Matthew 4: 12-23
Year B: Jonah 3: 1-10/ Psalm 62: 5-12/ 1 Corinthians 7: 29-31/Mark 1: 14-20
Year C: Nehemiah 8: 1-10/ Psalm 19/ 1 Corinthians 12: 12-31a/Luke 4: 14-21

Focus

Jesus announces his call and ministry mission by quoting the Prophet Isaiah. He goes on to announce that the time has come for change and begins to select disciples who have no prior experience, passion for ministry, or great depths of spiritual wisdom or maturity. It seems as if there is a random selection of those who make up his "seminary" class for the next three and a half years. Professional fishermen leave their boats. Two pair of brothers join the team. A tax collector and a couple of rebel rousers come along. The Light is yet calling. The world is beginning to see and experience the difference in his "good news." The Kingdom of God is made known as being near those who will hear.

Jonah gives us the first recorded testimony of one who was "called and appointed" to a mission ministry and refused to go! What are the "big fish," who swallow those who dare to run from God today? How do we announce "good news" to our worst enemies? Jonah was called to "twinkle" for God, and went in the opposite direction! Is it required of us that our enemies "see" the Christ Light in our response to them? The season of Epiphany calls the world to catch flashes of Christ in the way we walk the talk of salvation's "gift" given to us in Jesus Christ.

Visual Aids

(See notes on prior pages)

Call to Worship

Leader: Jonah, God is calling you to accountability!

People: We have come to worship. There is no Jonah in our midst!

Leader: Jonah, God is calling you to accountability!

People: We have gathered in this place with those like us to offer God thanks and praise.

Leader: Jonah, God is calling you to accountability!

People: We don't want to hear about "those people, out there". This is our time. This is our sacred space. For today, we need encouragement for ourselves.

Leader: Jonah, God is calling you to accountability! "Those people" are your assignment!

People: Lord, the Jonah in us wants to run. But, we have come to offer you praise. Feed us in this hour so that we might feed others when we leave. (Trumpet For Zion, B)

Musical Suggestions for Epiphany 3

Hymns for the Day

Title	AAHH	AME	AMEZ	LEVS	LMGM	YL	HG
A Charge to Keep I Have (BOYLSTON)	468	•	439	•	•	•	•
A Charge to Keep I Have (ST. THOMAS)	•	242	•	•	•	•	•
Come, Said Jesus' Sacred Voice	•	•	395	•	•	•	•
Here Am I	466	•	•	•	•	•	•
If Jesus Goes with Me	•	•	•	•	•	497	•
Jesus Is Tenderly Calling	351	239	411	•	•	303	•
O Zion, Haste Thy Mission	•	566	380	•	•	496	•
Softly and Tenderly	347	261	413	101	175	282	•
Wherever He Leads, I'll Go	•	•	•	•	•	370	•

Spirituals	AAHH	AME	AMEZ	LEVS	LMGM	YL	HG
Done Made My Vow	•	•	•	123	285	•	•

Gospel Selections	AAHH	AME	AMEZ	LEVS	LMGM	YL	HG
Only What You Do for Christ	548	•	•	•	286	•	•
Yes, Lord	667	•	•	•	284	title	•

Anthems

Let this Mind be in You *Lee Hoiby*
Good News *Jane Marshall*
Jonah *Dale Wood*

Spirituals

Witness *arr. Jack Halloran*
  (no. 20 in *The Oxford Book of Spirituals*, pp.155-167)
Don't You Let Nobody Turn You 'Round *arr. Lena J. McLin*
  (no. 23 in *The Oxford Book of Spirituals*, pp. 184-193)

Gospel Selections

Purpose in Your Heart *Carol Antrom*
It's My Desire *Freda Pullen Bagley/ Horace Clarence Boyer*

Organ Music

If Thou But Suffer God to Guide Thee, BWV 647 *J. S. Bach*
I Want to Walk as a Child of the Light *Wayne F. Wold* (from *Augsburg Organ Library–Epiphany*)
I Want Jesus to Walk with Me *Raymond Henry* (from *I'll Fly Away*)

Epiphany 4

Appropriate Banner and Altar Colors: Green
Year A: Micah 6: 1-8/ Psalm 15/ 1 Corinthians 1: 18-31/ Matthew 5: 1-12
Year B: Deuteronomy 18: 15-20/ 1 Corinthians 8: 1-13/ Mark 1: 21-28
Year C: Jeremiah 1: 4-10/ Psalm 71: 1-6/ 1 Corinthians 13: 1-13/ Luke 4: 21-30

Focus

Every scripture points us toward the great hymn of The Church known as *The Gift of Love.* "Though I may speak with bravest fire, and have the gift to all inspire, and have not love, my words are vain, as sounding brass and hopeless gain. Though I may give all I possess, and striving so my love to profess, but not be given, by love within, the profit soon turns strangely thin. Come, Spirit come, our hearts control, our spirits long to be made whole. Let inward love guide every deed, by this we worship and are freed."* These words of Hal Hopson echo the Corinthian message of Paul to a group of people who knew the talk, but did not walk the walk!

The message of the Corinthians is a call to unity. In the days in which we live, with racial tensions across the world, it is a prime opportunity for the Black Church to deal with both ecumenical and cross-cultural relationships. The Church at Corinth was a gifted congregation of well-intentioned people. Yet they were some of the most difficult people to pastor. They required Paul to deal with them strongly, to call them to task, and to give them a challenging definition of love. As African Americans, we find ourselves struggling to deal with the word "love." In the ancient world, there were three different words for love: Eros, familia, and agape. Eros refers to sexual love, familia is another word for family, and agape means spirtual love.

Just before we enter the celebration of Black History across America, the subject of agape, or that God-type love, would be a centering point for how we need to respond to the rest of the world! For God "loves" the racist, the bigot, and the segregationist just as much as God loves us! And God is yet looking, seeking, and searching for us, called Christian, to represent!

---

* © 1972, Hope Puplishing Co., Carol Stream, Illinois

VISUAL ARTS

Now is the time to focus on the development of an altar that will reflect your Black History theme. One suggestion is to do a progressive altar that starts with Africa and The Middle Passage and add to it each week items depicting our movements out of the South. Urban Ministries does a yearly series for Vacation Bible School, which contains wonderful art renderings of Black characters. A Moment in Black History should be part of every gathering this month, teaching our history and culture to the youth who are charged with telling our story to the generations that will follow.

BENEDICTION

Leader: Anyone who loves God is known and claimed by God!

People: Anyone who loves God also loves the people of God!

Leader: Name the people that God does not love!

People: There are none we can name; for God is love!

Leader: As lights of God, we have no choice but to love every neighbor as we love ourselves. Go into the world. God who is Love, Jesus who is Savior, and The Holy Spirit's Power; go with us to make us visible in the whole wide world.

People: Hallelujah and Amen!

Responsive Reading: The Community's: Lament (Psalms 86)

Leader: All-Seeing/All-Knowing God, our tears are before you day and night. Heed our petitions, answer when we cry.

People: Our spirit is troubled, we are weighed down with grief. Oftentimes we feel that we do not matter to you, that we are invisible and inconsequential in the world.

Leader: The issue of abandonment is ever painful for us. And when we seek your interventions and cannot see your face, we are simply overwhelmed.

People: Have you counted us as insignificant? Is our status, as so-called minorities, and our dark coloring of no matter to even you? You made us, you called us, we have gathered in your Name. We are here—but where are you?

Leader: There is nothing solid about our existence. Chaos and confusion is everywhere. When we feel we have made a significant gain, we are pushed further back in other areas of life. We call out to you and you do not answer! We cry, and your comfort is not!

People: We seek your pity and even you are counted among the indifferent! Is your Word really true? Is your counsel available? Do you honestly provide a balm for broken hearts and wounded spirits?

Leader: We are exhausted with trying; trying to do your will, trying to remain faithful, trying to see possibilities in the world's madness; trying to sing when the melody is gone; trying not to tell a story which is filled with an evil world and an absent God!

People: We lift our hands, and our arms are like lead. We open our mouths, and our tongues are like brass. We want to open our hearts, but the pain of rejection lingers so long! We want to believe in the Church, but where is the salvation for the neglected and the forgotten?

Leader: "Why us?" we cry, and there is no response. "How much more?" we inquire, and another blow slams us against the wall. "How long?" we beg, and the silence mocks us!

People: And, yet we stand. Waiting. Seeking. Longing. We know you have come before on behalf of the oppressed. You are the God who comes! So, we will wait for you!

(Trumpet For Zion, A)

Musical Suggestions for Epiphany 4

Hymns for the Day

Title	AAHH	AME	AMEZ	LEVS	LMGM	YL	HG
Blest Be the Tie that Binds	341	522	493	•	•	34	•
I Am Praying for You	350	329	•	168	288	457	•
In Christ There Is No East or West (MCKEE)	399	557	230	62	301	•	•
Love Lifted Me	504	461	429	198	•	425	•
Make Me a Blessing	•	•	•	158	•	356	•
The Gift of Love	522	•	409	•	•	•	•
The Love of God	•	•	•	•	•	47	•
They'll Know We Are Christians	•	•	683	•	•	•	•

Spirituals	AAHH	AME	AMEZ	LEVS	LMGM	YL	HG
Walk Together Children	541	•	•	•	•	•	•

Gospel Selections	AAHH	AME	AMEZ	LEVS	LMGM	YL	HG
Koinoia	579	•	•	•	•	•	•
Unity	338	•	•	•	•	•	•
We Are One	323	•	•	•	•	•	•

Anthems

God So Loved the World *Carl J. Nygard, Jr.*
God Is Love *Ralph Manuel*
Many Gifts, One Spirit *Allen Pote*
The King of Love My Shepherd Is *Harry Rowe Shelley*

Gospel Selections

Do You Possess God's Love? *Carol Antrom*
The Love of God *Lena McLin*

Organ Music

I Love Thee, My Lord *George Shearing*
Prelude in C *Charles Callahan*
Love Divine, All Loves Excelling *Ralph Vaughn Williams* (from *Augsburg Organ Library–Epiphany*)
I've Just Come from the Fountain *Richard Billingham* (from *Seven Reflections on African American Spirituals*)

Litany for Black History Month

Leader: In the Beginning was the Black Church, and the Black Church was with the Black Community.

People: The Black Church was in the Beginning with Black people and all things were made through the Black Church.

Leader: Without the Black Church, was not anything made that was made.

People: In the Black Church was life, and the life was the light of the Black People.

Leader: The Black Church still shines in the world, and the world has not overcome it.

People: Born in the agony of slavery and tyranny, the Black Church rose as the symbol of hope for every tomorrow.

Leader: There was hope for freedom in the Black Church.

People: There was hope for a better tomorrow in the Black Church.

Leader: There was the hope for deliverance from oppressors, NOW!, and not in the "sweet bye and bye!"

People: There was hope for a new day, a new beginning, a fresh start and "a building, not made with human hands."

Leader: Our hope is yet alive!

People: Our faith is yet firm!

Leader: The God of the Oppressed is our reality!

People: The Invisible Institution is visible and viable in and through us.

Leader: The Black Church continues to be the heartbeat of our communities.

People: And the High God of the Ancestors remains at the heart of the Black Church. Thanks be unto God for our heritage, our history, and our hope.

*First five stanzas taken from *Quest for a Black Theology*,
Gardiner & Roberts, Pilgrim Press
(Trumpet For Zion, A)

CALL TO WORSHIP

Leader: We gather that the Word of Life might encourage and enrich our hearts.

People: We come that our children might learn of God's intervention in our lives.

Leader: We assemble to rehearse our faith story, to name our heroes and heroines, and to give praise and worship to The Eternal.

People: The God of the Diaspora, Black, Dark, and Silent, is worthy of our worship and our praise.

Epiphany 5

Appropriate Banner and Altar Colors: Green
Year A: Isaiah 58: 1-12/ Psalm 112: 1-10/ 1 Corinthians 2: 1-16/ Matthew 5: 13-20
Year B: Isaiah 40: 21-31/Psalm 147:1-11, 20/ 1 Corinthians 9: 16-23/ Mark 1: 29-29
Year C: Isaiah 61: 1-13/ Psalm 138/ 1 Corinthians 15: 1-11/ Luke 5: 1-11

Because The Light of The World has come, all Hebrew scriptures focus on the comfort passages of Isaiah. The days of giving justice to others is God's call to The Chosen People. God demands a fast, not from food, but from withholding good from others. This is a serious call to people who have gotten so accustomed to being on the receiving end of life! These who feel abandoned and left by God are charged to show God's presence in their time of suffering and sorrow. They were called to be Lights! A light has no purpose but to shine. Evil cannot put out the Light of God! When Isaiah finally came to understand the holiness of God and heard the angelic beings singing, "Holy, Holy, Holy," He cried out, like we need to do, "Woe is me!" Which turns into, "Here I am, send me!" Can we be trusted to be sent to some of the worst situations, worst opportunities, and worst employment scenarios to shine forth as Light?

The Light of The World comes calling followers to be lights that sit atop a hill, salt preserving the world from the domination of sin, touching the sick, healing, performing miracles, and teaching fishermen to catch both fish and souls as his ministry takes off with passion. The Good News reinforces the Corinthians passages that attack human reason and proclaim the work of Jesus Christ. It was the Wisdom of The Ages, not human intellect and knowledge, that permitted the professional fishermen to return to "barren" waters after fishing all night and catching nothing. Going back again and again is a word to the wise! The nets begin to break when they heed the Masters command to launch out in the deep. Are we fishing too close to our "shores?" Who are some of the Black history makers who played the game of "repeat" many times before success? How did they allow their light to shine in such a restrictive and repressive era? What lessons do they teach us today?

Doxology for Black History Month

Praise God ye dark ones of the land
Sing praise for The Ancients sustaining hand
For all these gifts we have to share
Sing praise for God's blessings everywhere!
(Trumpet For Zion, A)

Visual Arts

In many congregations, this will be Communion Sunday. It is suggested that you ask different folks in the congregation to lend the altar their old-fashioned kerosene lamps for use. This was one of Harriet Tubman's primary signals as she came seeking those who wanted to go to a place of freedom. Lamps were also indicators of where your family sat in the earlier churches before electric lights. If your family was absent, your pew would be dark. The lamps will be a helpful reminder that "WE" are the lights of the world! The ministry of Jesus has been left to our hands. (See *AA Heritage Hymnal* for Litanies)

Musical Suggestions for Epiphany 5

Hymns for the Day

Title	AAHH	AME	AMEZ	LEVS	LMGM	YL	HG
God Is My Strong Salvation	495	•	•	•	•	•	•
Hail to the Brightness of Zion's Glad Morning	•	•	385	•	•	•	•
Holy, Holy, Holy	329	25	1	•	78	11	•
I Surrender All	396	251	490	133	235	319	•
In Me	452	•	•	•	•	•	•
Jesus, the Light of the World	217	112	111	•	•	•	•
Lead, Kindly Light (LUX BENIGNA)	501	•	67	•	•	•	•
Lead, Kindly Light (SANDON)	502	•	•	•	•	•	•
Take Time to Be Holy	•	286	467	•	•	336	•
Walk in the Light	•	524	485	•	•	•	•

Spirituals	AAHH	AME	AMEZ	LEVS	LMGM	YL	HG
This Little Light of Mine	549	•	617	•221	190	•	•

Gospel Selections	AAHH	AME	AMEZ	LEVS	LMGM	YL	HG
In the Beauty of Holiness	106	•	•	•	•	•	•
Shine on Me	527	•	•	•	•	•	•
Siyahamba	164	•	•	•	•	•	•
The Lord Is My Light	160	•	•	58	132	•	•
What a Mighty God We Serve	478	•	•	•	•	•	•

Anthems

Send Out Thy Light *Charles Gounod*   God Is Light *Paul Bouman*

Organ Music

We are Marching in the Light of God *Robert Buckley Farlee* (from *Augsburg Organ Library–Epiphany*)

Prelude sur l'introit de l'Epiphanie *Maurice Durufle* (from *Augsburg Organ Library–Epiphany*)

In Thee is Gladness, BWV 615 *Johann S. Bach*

Christ is the World's Light *J. Bert Carlson* (from *Augsburg Organ Library–Epiphany*)

Epiphany 6

Appropriate Banner and Altar Colors: Green
Year A: Deuteronomy 30:15-20/Psalm 119: 1-8/ 1 Corinthians 3: 1-9/ Matthew 5: 21-37
Year B: 2 Kings 5: 1-14/ Psalm 30/ 1 Corinthians 9: 24-27/ Mark 1: 40-45
Year C: Jeremiah 17: 5-10/ Psalm 1/ 1 Corinthians 15: 12-20/ Luke 6: 17-26

Focus

How do we trust God after all we have been through? Israel asked this question, and Jeremiah told them not to place any confidence in systems or institutions. Their trust in God would ground them in the times of anguish, perplexity, and distress, causing living water to spring up for reassurance and hope. A Black Church Conference was called asking the same question. "How can we be Black and Christian?" Interesting question to consider this month. Are the Biblical answers as reassuring for us today?

How do we trust a Jesus who heals a leper who is cast out of community and then tells those who are in community that, "You are blessed when you are poor, hungry, weeping, and despised?" What sacrifices we have made to "Move On Up To The East Side" and discover Jesus saying, "Woe to you who are rich, full, laughing, and respected!" These are not our community values. We are the wearers of Kente, gold, and diamonds. While we have attained the big houses, the good jobs, and the respect of our peers, what do we do with these values of The Teacher? While "bling, bling" and ganster rides have our youth with wide open hands and searching eyes, how do we teach about the delayed gratification for which The Ancestors gave their very lives?

Visual Arts

The altar decor might offer some of the items that Black people have discovered and patented such as the comb, the mail box drop slot, the hot comb, and of course many bags of peanuts! A book of little known facts about African Americans would offer the opportunity for youth to see just how much they don't know about their history!

Benediction

Leader: The God of The Ancestors bless you.
People: The Ancient of Days enfold you.
Leader: The Light of Glory shine upon you.
People: The Darkness of Growth give you sound sleep.
Leader: The Help of The Ages goes with us.
People: The Hope of Tomorrow bids us "Come".
Leader: Let's leave to walk in this faith and confidence.
People: Amen! (Trumpet For Zion, A)

(See *AA Heritage Hymnal* for Litanies)

Musical Suggestions for Epiphany 6

Hymns for the Day

Title	AAHH	AME	AMEZ	LEVS	LMGM	YL	HG
God Will Take Care of You	137	437	77	183	·	76	·
I Know Who Holds Tomorrow	415	446	48	·	187	124	·
O God, Our Help in Ages Past	170	61	81	·	230	15	·
Only Trust Him	369	422	·	·	·	470	·
The Solid Rock	385	·	·	·	·	103	·
Trust and Obey	380	377	443	205	·	334	·

Spirituals	AAHH	AME	AMEZ	LEVS	LMGM	YL	HG
I Will Trust in the Lord	391	·	·	193	232	333	·

Gospel Selections	AAHH	AME	AMEZ	LEVS	LMGM	YL	HG
All My Help Comes	370	·	·	·	·	·	·
He Knows Just How Much	·	·	76	·	254	389	·
I've Got a Feelin'	313	·	·	·	252	·	·
My Heavenly Father Watches	144	·	84	59	·	139	·
The Beatitudes	81	·	·	·	·	·	·
Through It All	·	·	·	·	228	71	·
Yes, God Is Real	162	361	53	209	226	128	·

Anthems

In God We Trust #55 LEVS   The Beatitudes H. R. Evans
O Lord, in Thee Have I Trusted G. F. Handel

Spirituals

I Will Trust in the Lord *Undine Smith Moore*   My Soul's Been Anchored in the Lord *Moses Hogan*
My Soul's Been Anchored in De Lord *Glenn L. Burleigh*

Organ Music

The Lord Will Make a Way *Raymond Henry* (from *I'll Fly Away*)

He Knows Just How Much We Can Bear *Raymond Henry* (from *I'll Fly Away*)

My Hope is Built on Nothing Less *David Cherwien* (from *Interpretations, Book IX*)

Epiphany 7

Appropriate Banner and Altar Colors: Green
Year A: Leviticus 19: 1-18, Psalm 119: 33-40/ 1 Corinthians 3: 10-23/ Matthew 5: 38-48
Year B: Isaiah 43: 18-25/ Psalm 41/ 1 Corinthians 1: 18-22/ Mark 2: 1-12
Year C: Genesis 45: 3-11/ Psalm 37, 1-11, 39-40/1 Corinthians 15: 35-38, 42-50/Luke 6: 27-38

Focus

The "Holiness Codes" and treating brothers and sisters in manners that exhibit agape love is the call throughout the scriptures. "I am the Lord, your God who makes holy...treat your neighbor as family!" The neighbors to Israel were often the same folks who had enslaved them or made their lives bitter in other ways. Yet Joseph's brothers treated him worst than a bondservant by selling him into slavery in Egypt. Some twenty years later, when the man who saves their lives with needed food reveals himself as "Your brother, Joseph," there was pandemonium and bedlam. Sometimes our worst enemies are not "those people!" How do we treat those who mistreat us within the family?

Jesus picks up this theme with his teachings of The Beatitudes, which are the upside-down values that The Church of God is called to live. We are told to love, serve, and pray for our enemies. We are called to go the extra mile. We are admonished to pray for those who have mistreated us the most. We are commanded to not take retaliatory action against those who do us physical harm. This must have sounded outrageous to the first hearers of This Word. They were looking for a Messiah on a white horse, who would kick tail and take names for all the damage done to them. They had real serious problems with this teaching, which has not gone out of style. How would this "law" of Jesus, as enacted throughout Dr. Martin Luther King, Jr.'s non-violent campaign for Civil Rights, be treated today with the current levels of violence all around us? It's a question to ponder.

Visual Arts

We are halfway through the month and should be about ready to focus on 20th Century heroes and heroines. The music, films, and advertisements we have done that uplift the positive contributions need to be displayed. Old seventy-eights, a Victrola, and eight tracks need to put in an appearance on the altar. For all we are, we offer to God as our light to the world.

Musical Suggestions for Epiphany 7

Hymns for the Day

Title	AAHH	AME	AMEZ	LEVS	LMGM	YL	HG
For Healing of the Nations	•	•	391	•	•	•	•
God of Love and God of Power	•	•	51	•	•	•	•
Help Us Forgive, Forgiving Lord	•	•	•	•	•	•	17
Let There Be Peace on Earth	498	•	384	•	300	505	•
Make Me a Blessing	•	•	•	158	•	356	•
Throw Out the Lifeline	•	245	677	•	•	483	•
We've a Story to Tell to the Nations	•	•	388	•	•	•	•

Spirituals	AAHH	AME	AMEZ	LEVS	LMGM	YL	HG
Come and Go with Me	596	•	•	•	250	•	•
I Know the Lord Laid His Hand	360	352	52	131	243	•	•
Jesus Is a Rock in a Weary Land	222	•	•	•	•	•	•
Lord, I Want to Be a Christian	463	282	606	138	119	277	•
Lord, Make Me More Holy	632	•	•	•	222	•	•

Anthems

Lord, Make Me an Instrument of Thy Peace *John Rutter*

Striving After God *Undine Smith Moore*

Gospel Selections

Lord, Make Me an Instrument of Thy Peace *arr. Roger Holland, III*

Healing *Richard Smallwood*

Organ Music

Maryton *Noel Da Costa* (*Anthology of African American Organ Music*, Vol. 3)

O Zion, Haste *Mark Sedio* (from *Augsburg Organ Library–Epiphany*)

We Are All One in Mission *Mark Sedio* (from *Augsburg Organ Library–Epiphany*)

Epiphany 8

Appropriate Banner and Altar Colors: Green
Year A: Isaiah 49: 8-16/ Psalm 131/ 1 Corinthians 4: 1-5/ Matthew 6: 24-34
Year B: Hosea 2: 14-20/ Psalm 103: 1-13, 22/ 2 Corinthians 3: 1-6/ Mark 2: 13-22
Year C: Isaiah 55: 10-13/ Psalm 92: 1-15/ 1 Corinthians 15: 51-58/ Luke 6: 39-49

Focus

God is faithful! Every Scripture reminds us of this fact. We are the unfaithful ones! We get so busy building lives, seeking fortunes, and being swallowed up by the fast and furious pace of the world in order to be "successful" that we move away from God. And when crisis come, we feel that God has left us! Yet in love, in mercy, and with long suffering, God has "married" The Church! We are adulterous! We are the wanderers! We are the ones who dare to seek a better lover who does not require as much from us! For we want discipleship without discipline. We want rituals and routines without the rigors demanded of disciples. We want to do it our way, set our own pace, and hear sermons that comfort our lifestyles and make us feel happy in our sin! However, new life that comes through the perfect sacrifice of Jesus Christ and his shed blood will not allow us to sit in our comfortable sins too long! The Son of God has authority to forgive sins. But, even while we are far off, doing things our way, someone somewhere is praying for us. And God, who is faithful and has established us, bought us, paid the brides' price for us, and commissioned us as Lights to the World, expects us to straighten up, come "home," and minister to "the little ones!"

Visual Aids

Depending upon the passages selected to end this journey through Epiphany, the theme of light shows up in many diverse ways. There is first the light of freedom, which can be reflected through old lanterns and photos of the Underground Railroad sights. There is the light of love in the face of brides and grooms, parents welcoming infants, and the steady love of older couples. There is the light of justice in the scales that America uses to indicate equality of standards and of course in the soaring eagle. And pictures of teachers sitting and passing along knowledge to our little ones is always a joy- filled de-Light!

Call to Worship

Leader: We gather that the Word of Life might encourage and enrich our hearts.
People: We come that our children might learn of God's intervention in our lives.
Leader: We assemble to rehearse our faith story, to name our heroes and heroines, and to give praise and worship to The Eternal.
People: The God of the Diaspora, Black, Dark, and Silent, is worthy of our worship and our praise.

Musical Suggestions for Epiphany 8

Hymns for the Day

Title	AAHH	AME	AMEZ	LEVS	LMGM	YL	HG
Be Still, My Soul	135	426	458	•	163	96	•
Great Is Thy Faithfulness	158	84	80	189	242	122	•
Hope of Ages, Thou Art God	•	•	650	•	•	•	•
How Firm a Foundation	146	433	309	•	102	54	•
Jesus Is Always There	•	•	634	•	•	•	•
O God, Our Help in Ages Past	170	61	81	•	230	15	•
Standing on the Promises	373	424	260	•	•	105	•
The Solid Rock	385	•	•	•	•	103	•
Tis So Sweet to Trust	368	440	508	108	236	102	•
What a Friend We Have (CONVERSE)	431	323	282	109	214	342	•

Spirituals	AAHH	AME	AMEZ	LEVS	LMGM	YL	HG
Jesus Is a Rock in a Weary Land	222	•	•	•	•	•	•

Gospel Selections	AAHH	AME	AMEZ	LEVS	LMGM	YL	HG
God Is	134	•	•	•	•	•	•
God Never Fails	159	•	•	•	224	110	•
He Brought Me Out	509	•	•	•	•	432	•
He's Done So Much for Me	511	•	•	•	•	•	•
He's Sweet I Know	510	•	•	•	•	137	•
Jesus, I'll Never Forget	•	•	•	•	•	345	•
We've Come This Far by Faith	412	•	•	208	225	395	•

Anthems

God of Grace and God of Glory *Paul T. Langstron*

Spirituals

Jesus Is a Rock *arr. John W. Work*
 (No. 4 in *The Oxford Book of Spirituals* pp. 25-36)

Organ Music

Give Me Jesus *Richard Billingham* (from *Seven Reflections on African American Spirituals*)
Great is Thy Faithfulness *Dan Miller*
In Christ There is No East or West *Charles Callahan*

Transfiguration Sunday

Appropriate Banner and Altar Colors: White or Gold
Year A: Exodus 24: 12-18/ Psalm 2/ 2 Peter 1: 16-21/ Matthew 17: 1-9
Year B: 2 Kings 2: 1-12/ Psalm 50: 1-6/ 2 Corinthians 4: 3-6/ Mark 9: 2-9
Year C: Exodus 34: 29-35/ Psalm 99/ 2 Corinthians 3: 12-4: 2/ Luke 9: 28-43

Focus

This is the day that the disciples see the "great change" in Jesus, their teacher. His face changes. His clothes change. His environment changes. And the folks he's with suddenly change. With Jesus stands a representative of the Laws, Moses, and the prophets, Elisha. A voice thunders out of heaven indicating that The Beloved dwells upon the earth. And scared disciples begin to talk foolishly. "Let's stay here in the glory and build three temples." What do we do when we actually experience God's glory? What is our response to the "great changes" we know have happened in our own lives? How do we express our thanks for the transformation? And how do we leave the "glory moment" to return to the work in the mundane world? A good question to ask, wrestle with, and ponder is, "What is the change, the transformation and the new deal of your life?" Many of us are "stuck" in our places, but "The Glory" has been gone!

Responsive Reading: Based on Psalms 2

Leader: It's the same old story! Dark skinned people around the globe continue to be mistreated, cast aside, and conspired against by those in power.

People: Why do entire nations scheme against us? What makes hate groups continue to devise methods for our eradication? Where is our change?

Leader: We are continually removed from power centers, forced to work for the lowest possible pay, stripped of political influence through redlining and gerrymandering, viewed and regarded as sub-human, while we are the people who possess the Secret of Joy!

People: The God of Many Deliverances laughs at the oppressors. In wrath and fury, the vengeance of God will be unleashed against them. We long for our change!

Leader: The Friend of Zion has come and identified with the marginal and oppressed.

People: The Chosen of God is in Zion! We have been established as the salt of the earth, the light of the world, and a nation that cannot be hidden. We must be changed!

Leader: The nations of the earth sprang forth from our loins. The ends of the earth belong to us. Poverty shall be broken and injustice will crumble like a potter's vessel. The day of change approaches!

People: When we come into power, let Wisdom work perfectly in us. We will serve The First and The Last with awe. Our hope and our wholeness are complete in the God who works change in us!

Altar Focus

As the drama of Lent unfolds, with its journey toward the cross and resurrection, the altar should set the tempo for meditation and reflection. A Lenten garden might be a possibility for you. Local florists will gather the necessary plants and rent them for the season. Included should be any plant that will remind us of the Garden of Gethsemane, the place where Jesus spent his hours anticipating death for us.

Stalks of wheat and vines should be heavily emphasized, as Jesus is the Bread of Life and the Vine from which we are nourished. Wheat was most likely the most important crop in that period. A huge rock or simulated boulder should be included to remind us of wise and foolish persons who select to build their faith on rock or sand. Perhaps a quiet waterfall might be included so that your altar would attract members during the weeks ahead, as a sacred spot for stopping to take a drink from the Fountain of Life, which never runs dry. Let your imagination flow and allow the artistry of your worship committee to make the garden one to remember. If you place lilies around the altar the day before Easter, the beauty will be striking!

This period of the church's year also includes Women's History Month in March. International Women's History Day is March 8. You will do your congregation a great service as you highlight the Biblical and historical contributions of women throughout the month.

(See *AA Heritage Hymnal* for Litanies)

MUSICAL SUGGESTIONS FOR TRANSFIGURATION SUNDAY

HYMNS FOR THE DAY

Title	AAHH	AME	AMEZ	LEVS	LMGM	YL	HG
Jesus, Take Us to the Mountain	•	•	•	•	•	•	131
Since Jesus Came Into My Heart	499	403	•	•	•	442	•
Spirit Song	321	•	•	118	•	•	•
The Chosen Tree, On Mountain Height	•	•	252	•	•	•	•
Transform Us As You, Transfigured	•	•	•	•	•	•	149

Spirituals	AAHH	AME	AMEZ	LEVS	LMGM	YL	HG
I Know I've Been Changed	•	357	•	•	•	•	•
I Know the Lord Laid His Hands	360	352	52	131	243	•	•
I'm Gonna Live So God Can Use Me	•	358	•	•	•	•	•

ANTHEMS

Christ Upon the Mountain Peak *Paul Bouman*
From the Eastern Mountain *Healey Willan*
Jesus, Take Us to the Mountain *Carl Schalk*

Transfiguration *Joel Martinson*
Transfiguration *Alec Wynton*

SPIRITUALS

I Know I Been Changed *arr. Roy L. Belfield, Jr.*

GOSPEL SELECTIONS

Changed *Walter Hawkins*   Changed *Eddie Robinson*

ORGAN MUSIC

3. Spiritual: 'Round About the Mountain *Noel DaCosta* (*Spiritual Set*)

LENT

The Season of Lent

We become pilgrims on the forty-day journey, seeking our way out of the wilderness of sin in the season of Lent. It is a serious period of spiritual discipline as we either give up something pleasant or take on a new mission to enable others. Lent is our individual struggle to subdue our flesh and to wrestle with the sin issue, which tempts us so readily.

The early church prepared new members and catechumens for Easter Sunday baptism. There was an intense year of being indoctrinated into the faith community. Both instructors and students of the faith fasted, prayed, studied, and made themselves more consciously aware of the sacrifice of Jesus Christ.

The Israelites wandered forty years in the wilderness. Jesus spent forty days and nights struggling with Satan in the wilderness. We will journey through our own forty-day wilderness, knowing that resurrection is on the way.

It is good to note that Sundays are not included in the forty-day Lenten period. Each Sunday worship experience is a re-enactment of the resurrection!

Ash Wednesday

Appropriate Banner and Altar Colors: Purple

Year A, B, and C: Joel 2: 1-7, Psalm 51: 1-17/ 2 Corinthians 5: 20b-6: 10 Matthew 6: 1-6, 16-21

Focus

The theme for this day is remembering that we are the very ones who celebrated Christ last Palm Sunday, and then slowly but surely walked away in self-indulgent lifestyles since the victory shouts on Easter Sunday morning! "Christ is risen! Christ is risen indeed!" What a shout of joy we shared. However, since that time, we have continued to follow the rituals and forgotten the true reason that we do what we do! So Ash Wednesday comes to assist us in remembering our sin. Ash Wednesday comes to help us recall that we are earthly flesh who, with the best of intentions, still leave the perfect will of God. So the tradition calls for the palms that "we" waved last Palm Sunday to be burned, and those ashes are spread upon our foreheads to remind us of whose we are; people of the Most High God, called to fast, weep, and mourn as we return wholeheartedly "home."

There are three personal acts of piety that people of God have participated in down the ages: the acts of charity or almsgiving, the act of prayer, and the act of fasting or giving up food that we especially like. For many years, Catholic's gave up meats and ate only fish on Fridays as a method of evidencing personal piety or good works toward God. Most of us are not aware of the reason that Friday Fish Fries continue in our communities. The Catholic Church is no longer tied to this particular "fast," but we are!

This period of remembering that we are "flesh" who quickly forget God is a call to giving up that which will draw our attention away from God. And it is a time of taking on additional ministry opportunities that allow us to reflect upon God's graciousness in our personal life. This is usually a short worship service of scripture reading, a time of altar confession, and the marking of ashes upon the forehead or hands. We are now ready to begin the Lenten Journey with Jesus to Calvary.

Suggestion for "trial" worship instead of a mid-week Bible Study, (Call to Worship: Read the Joel passage):

Have children dressed as clowns come in with garden implements and dirty hands. They are silent as they walk from the rear, speaking and smiling at each row. They notice the Cross at the altar and make attempts to kneel. But their dirty hands prevent them. One of the adult leaders, dressed as a clown, comes and offers each child a handiwipe. They cleanse their hands and go kneel, signifying clean hearts before God. The children offer each member of the congregation a handiwipe. A time of silent prayer is offered.

Call to Confession

Use Psalm passage as responsive confession. Allow time for silent confession.

Words of Assurance

For our sake, God made Jesus, who knew no sin to be sin so that in him we might become the righteousness of God. See, now is the acceptable time. And with our confession, now is the day of salvation. This is mighty good news.

Imposition of Ashes

If last year's palms are not handy, a local florist or Bible bookstore will have them available for purchase. Make clear to the congregation that Ash Wednesday is our occasion to remember our mortality and help us prepare for the six-week journey to the Resurrection Event, which is to come and mark us with eternal life!

Offertory Invitation

We will not put any obstacle in anyone's way, so that no fault may be found with our ministry, but as servants of God we have commended ourselves in every way. We give so that others may come and experience new life in Christ.

Offertory Praise

God of all, your love towards us is so marvelous. We thank you for all you have given us. We rejoice in this opportunity to be poor enough in spirit that we gladly share to make others part of your Realm. We give because we recognize that we have nothing of ourselves, but with your great love, we possess everything!

Benediction

Leader: The journey to Calvary begins.

People: We commend ourselves to God.

Leader: The journey calls us to receive the grace of God for every facet of our lives.

People: We commend ourselves to God.

Leader: The journey will call for great endurance on our part.

People: We commend ourselves to God.

Leader: Take the journey enfolded by Love, Truth and Power. I commend each of us to God!

(Trumpet For Zion A)

MUSICAL SUGGESTIONS FOR ASH WEDNESDAY

HYMNS FOR THE DAY

Title	AAHH	AME	AMEZ	LEVS	LMGM	YL	HG
Forty Days and Forty Nights	•	•	•	•	42	•	•
From the River to the Desert	•	•	•	•	•	•	54
Have Thine Own Way, Lord	449	345	492	145	•	313	•
In Me	452	•	•	•	•	•	•
It Took a Miracle	155	•	•	•	•	452	•
Jesus, Keep Me Near the Cross	•	321	300	29	45	244	•
Lord Who Throughout These Forty Days	•	•	131	•	40	•	•
Lord, I Want to Live for Thee	433	•	•	173	124	•	•
Take Time to Be Holy	•	286	467	•	•	336	•
Thy Way, O Lord	444	311	•	•	39	•	•
Touch Me, Lord Jesus	274	334	•	•	•	•	•

Spirituals	AAHH	AME	AMEZ	LEVS	LMGM	YL	HG
Hush, Somebody's Calling My Name	556	•	•	128	262	•	•
I'm Gonna Live So God Can Use Me	•	358	•	•	•	•	•
Oh Lord, Have Mercy	448	•	•	•	•	•	•
Somebody's Knockin at Your Door	348	•	•	100	34	•	•

Gospel Selections	AAHH	AME	AMEZ	LEVS	LMGM	YL	HG
Give Me a Clean Heart	461	•	•	124	279	•	•
Lord, Have Mercy (Roberts)	655	•	•	•	•	•	•
Lord, Have Mercy (Walker)	656	•	•	•	•	8	•
Lord, Touch Me	•	•	•	•	158	•	•

ANTHEMS
Lord, I Want to Live for Thee *Arr. Leo Davis*   Have Mercy on Us, O My Lord *Aaron Copland*

SPIRITUALS
When I Was Sinking Down *arr. Hall Johnson*

GOSPEL SELECTIONS
Sanctify Me *V. Michael McKay*

ORGAN MUSIC
Ah Been in duh Storm So Long, Chillun! *arr. William Farley Smith* (from *Songs of Deliverance*)
Adagio and Fugue in F minor *Adolphus Hailstork*
Meditation on "Steal Away" *William Cooper*
Steal Away to Jesus *Raymond H. Haan*

The First Sunday of Lent

Appropriate Banner and Altar Colors: Purple
Year A: Genesis 2: 15-17; 3: 1-7/ Psalm 32/ Romans 5: 12-19/ Matthew 4: 1-11
Year B: Genesis 9: 8-17/ Psalm 25: 1-10/ 1 Peter 3: 18-22/ Mark 1: 9-15
Year C: Deuteronomy 26: 1-11/ Psalm 91: 1-2, 9-16/ Romans 10: 8-13/ Luke 4: 1-13

Focus

"Yield not to temptation, for yielding is sin," said the songwriter of old, reflecting upon the themes running through these passages. For it is the yielding that separates us from a holy and righteous God. Genesis takes us back to The Beginning and The Fall, while Deuteronomy tells us to recite the story of The Ancestors of the faith and remember how God has been faithful! Since God is faithful, we can willingly offer our first fruits or tithes. All the gospel passages are focused upon the wilderness experience of Jesus before he began "official" ministry. While in the human condition of hunger and weariness and wrestling with The Tempter, Jesus had to decide how he was going to take on his "assignment." Satan offered him prosperity, world power, and miracles. Notice that Jesus never argued that Satan was not the ruler of this world! Jesus simply gave the evil one the written words of scripture that he had committed to memory. And it is good to be reminded that even the devil quoted scripture too! Jesus did not yield to the Tempter's temptations. This is our working purpose during the season of Lent. We will not yield to temptation! The Holy Spirit is working on our behalf.

Call to Worship

Leader: The God of Covenant has arrived to settle the score.
People: The account will not be in our favor.
Leader: The God of The Beginning is here to work in the gardens of our hearts.
People: Weeds, thickets, and briars have covered God's first work!
Leader: The God of Covenant has made arrangements for removing all that is not quality fruit.
    The arrangements were made at Calvary.
People: The God of Covenant is faithful. We come to offer thanks and praise.

(See *AA Heritage Hymnal* for Litanies)

Musical Suggestions for The First Sunday of Lent

Hymns for the Day

Title	AAHH	AME	AMEZ	LEVS	LMGM	YL	HG
Jesus, Tempted in the Desert	•	•	•	•	•	•	65
Oh Love, How Deep	•	•	128	•	•	•	•
The Lily of the Valley	381	186	•	•	•	231	•
Does Jesus Care	428	442	•	•	•	393	•
Farther Along	376	355	522	187	•	•	•
Where Could I Go	432	•	•	•	•	•	•
Guide Me O Thou Great Jehovah (CWM RHONDDA)	138	52	82	•	•	•	•
Guide Me O Thou Great Jehovah (ZION)	140	53	681	•	•	•	•
Yield Not to Temptation	429	413	518	170	174	325	•
Jesus, Lover of My Soul (MARTYN)	453	253	293	79	169	37	•
Forty Days and Forty Nights	•	•	•	•	42	•	•
The Glory of These Forty Days	•	•	•	•	32	•	•

Spirituals	AAHH	AME	AMEZ	LEVS	LMGM	YL	HG
He Knows Just What I Need	358	•	•	•	•	•	•
I Want Jesus to Walk with Me	563	375	514	70	263	381	•
'Tis the Old Ship of Zion	349	•	612	•	•	494	•

Gospel Selections	AAHH	AME	AMEZ	LEVS	LMGM	YL	HG
Lead Me, Guide Me	474	378	•	194	168	•	•

Anthems
When I Survey the Wondrous Cross *arr. Gilbert Martin*
When I Survey the Wondrous Cross *John W. Work, III* (from *Isaac Watts Contemplates the Cross*)

Spirituals
Jesus Walked This Lonesome Valley *William Dawson*
We Shall Walk Through the Valley *Undine Smith Moore*
The Lily of the Valley *arr. Wendell P. Whalum* (no. 18 in *The Oxford Book of Spirituals*, pp. 141-146)

Gospel Selections
Don't Give Up Your Cross *Margaret Pleasant Douroux*
Nailed to the Cross *V. Michael McKay*

Organ Music
Ah'm Trubl'd in Mind! *William Farley Smith* (from *Songs of Deliverance*)
Once More, My Soul *George Shearing*
Choral Dorien *Jehan Alain* (from *Augsburg Organ Library–Lent*)

The Second Sunday of Lent

Appropriate Banner and Altar Colors: Purple
Year A: Genesis 12: 1-4a/ Psalm 121/ Romans 4: 1-5, 13-17/ John 3: 1-17
Year B: Genesis 17: 1-7, 15-16/ Psalm 22: 23-31/ Romans 4: 13-25/ Mark 8: 31-38
Year C: Genesis 15: 1-12, 17-18/ Psalm 27/ Philippians 3: 17-4: 1/ Luke 13: 31-35

Focus

The Word of God points us toward the Covenant, which was made available to us through Abram and Sarai. These are some people we need to look at closely. Why could The Sovereign God choose "old folks?" What was the purpose of having a barren couple leave home and begin a journey to "who knows where?" What were the terms of a covenant? What did Abram and Saria have to give in exchange for all that God promised them? It is normal that when two parties enter into a contract, they both offer something as collateral. Abram, whose name indicated that he came from a high position that he was leaving, couldn't take much with him in the days before United Van Lines! And Saria, the princess of her people, had not been able to conceive and was awfully concerned about this promise of God to make them the Ancestors of more than the stars and grains of sand! Lent is a good time to wrestle with the issue of grace greater than what we can ever repay! Lent is an ideal time to struggle with how we keep our part of the Covenant with God.

Call to Order

Leader: It's time for a worthy worship and the reading of the will.
People: We have come with no knowledge of a "will."
Leader: God has left us in the will. It's always been part of the Covenant.
People: We have come with the knowledge that we have broken the Covenant.
Leader: God knew that and made provisions through Jesus Christ in the will.
People: Thank God for a binding will that makes us heirs to every promise.
Leader: Thank God for the beneficence that made the Covenant possible.
People: We are ready. It's time for worthy worship. For we are in the will!
Leader: Thanks be unto our Covenant keeping God.

Musical Suggestions for The Second Sunday of Lent

Hymns for the Day

Title	AAHH	AME	AMEZ	LEVS	LMGM	YL	HG
A Charge to Keep I Have (BOYLSTON)	468	•	439	•	•	•	•
A Charge to Keep I Have (ST. THOMAS)	•	242	•	•	•	•	•
God of Grace and God of Glory	•	62	227	•	•	•	•
Joyful, Joyful We Adore Thee	120	75	11	•	197	17	•
My Faith Looks Up to Thee	456	415	468	88	221	127	•
Standing on the Promises	373	424	260	•	•	105	•
The Glory of These Forty Days	•	•	•	•	32	•	•

Spirituals	AAHH	AME	AMEZ	LEVS	LMGM	YL	HG
Let the Heaven Light Shine	630	•	•	174	189	•	•

Gospel Selections	AAHH	AME	AMEZ	LEVS	LMGM	YL	HG
El Shaddai	•	•	63	•	•	•	•
The Lord Is My Light	160	•	•	58	132	66	•

Anthems

O For a Faith *arr. Nathan Carter*
Let Mount Zion Rejoice *J.B. Herbert*
Thou Wilt Keep Him *Samuel S. Wesley*
God So Loved the World #237 YL
I Will Lift Up Mine Eyes *Leo Sowerby*
Canon on 'I Will Lift Up My Eyes to the Hills' *David Hurd*

Spirituals

Hold On! *arr. Jester Hairston*
Little Innocent Lamb *arr. Marshall Bartholomew*
Ain't Got Time to Die *Hall Johnson*
When I Was Sinking Down *Hall Johnson*

Organ Music

O Master, Let Me Walk with Thee *Noel Da Costa* (*Anthology of African American Organ Music,* Vol. 3)
Folk Tune *Percy W. Whitlock*
Jesus, Still Lead On *Paul Manz* (from *Augsburg Organ Library–Lent*)

The Third Sunday of Lent

Appropriate Banner and Altar Colors: Purple
Year A: Genesis 9:9-17/Psalm 25:1-10/1 Peter 3:18-22/ Mark 1: 9-15
Year B: Exodus 20: 1-17/ Psalm 19? 1 Corinthians 1: 18-25/ John 2: 13-22
Year C: Isaiah 55: 1-9/ Psalm 63: 1-8/ 1 Corinthians 10: 1-13/ Luke 13: 1-9

Focus

The Sovereign God has brought about the promises made to Abraham and Sarah. There is now a Jewish nation, yet they are wanderers who are in need of God's provisions and are rebellious against the Covenant. The free gift of Amazing Grace continues to call those who are willing to the eschatological banquet without need for any money, by a simple acceptance of the invitation to "Come! Buy! Eat!" Paul picks up on this theme of God's grace and reminds the young Church that the obligation to stand with those on the margins belongs to them! What foolishness it sounds like to them. Yet it was the divine design of God to take what seemed to be foolish, weak, barren, landless, old people to make a wise and strong people, called to be Lights to the world.

The Good News has those who oppose Jesus slipping in the darkness with questions for him that are answered with words of true mystery. The Temple's "wise man" simply cannot comprehend the spiritual component of humans. "How can this be?" It's a good question. How can it be that we, the few, are to care for the many? How can it be that the little we have is supposed to stretch through our tithes and offerings? How can it be that financial greed can be such a strong part of Church ethics when we remember that he stepped into "nothing" and created everything that exists? How can it be that the Church would dare to "rob" God and God's little ones when The Almighty fed the Ancestors in the desert and brought forth water from a rock? How can it be that Jesus encountered "separate but equal" quarters in The Temple when the Church began as a small group of those termed "minorities?" How can this be?

Call to Worship

Leader: This day we encounter a speaking God.
People: Speak Lord, your servants are listening.
Leader: As a matter of fact, our God uses many words to communicate with us.
People: Speak Lord, your servants want to hear.
Leader: The Commandments are not simple rules or nice suggestions, but ways of conducting our lives.
People: You have already spoken Lord! Give us grace, now, to hear and to obey.

(Trumpet B)

Musical Suggestions for The Third Sunday of Lent

Hymns for the Day

Title	AAHH	AME	AMEZ	LEVS	LMGM	YL	HG
And Can It Be that I Should Gain	·	459	·	·	·	·	·
Fill My Cup, Lord	447	·	340	·	·	359	·
My Soul, Be on Thy Guard (LABAN)	·	376	513	·	·	·	·
Rock of Ages	559	328	170	·	51	91	·
Think of His Goodness to You	269	·	·	204	·	79	·
Where Cross the Crowded Ways	·	561	378	·	·	·	·

Spirituals	AAHH	AME	AMEZ	LEVS	LMGM	YL	HG
Hush, Somebody's Calling My Name	556	·	·	128	262	·	·
I Want Jesus to Walk with Me	563	375	514	70	263	381	·
Somebody's Knockin' at Your Door	348	·	·	100	34	·	·

Gospel Selections	AAHH	AME	AMEZ	LEVS	LMGM	YL	HG
He's Sweet I Know	510	·	·	·	·	137	·
He's So Real	237	·	·	·	489	·	·
Sweeter Than the Day Before	·	·	·	·	227	489	·

Anthems

Ho! Everyone That Thirsteth *Will Macfarlane*

O Come, Every One that Thirsteth
  Mendelssohn/arr. Thomas Sheets

Amazing Grace *arr. Evelyn Simpson-Curenton*

Spirituals

Hush! Somebody's Callin' My Name
  arr. Brazeal Dennard

I Want Jesus *arr. Jester Hairston*

Jesus Walked this Lonesome Valley
  arr. William Dawson

I Want Jesus to Walk with Me *arr. Moses Hogan*

Gospel Selections

He Never Failed Me Yet *Robert Ray*

Organ Music

Ah, Jesus, Dear, Op. 122, No. 2 *Johannes Brahms*

Three Pieces for Organ *George Walker*

Toccata on "Amazing Grace" *J. Christopher Pardini*

Fourth Sunday In Lent

Appropriate Banner and Altar Colors: Purple
Year A: 1 Samuel 16: 1-3/ Psalm 23/ Ephesians 5: 8-14/ John 9: 1-41
Year B: Numbers 21: 4-9/ Psalm 107: 1-3, 17-22/ Ephesians 2: 1-10/ John 3: 14-21
Year C: Joshua 5: 9-12/ Psalm 32/ 2 Corinthians 5: 16-21/ Luke 15: 1-3, 11b-32

Focus

Psalm 23 is an excellent passage to preach from and sing about as we wander through the wilderness of Lent. For David did not write this Psalm while sitting in the splendor of the palace at Jerusalem! David did not have the luxury of dictating to the scribe, who took down every kingly word with pride! David wrote this prayer petition as he was running from Saul, The King who was trying diligently to take his life. David wrote this Psalm to encourage his soul. For he had been lost in his father's house as Jesse paraded all of his elder sons before Samuel, the prophet! They had forgotten about "little" David, who was out tending sheep and killing bears and lions to protect them. After being anointed king, things didn't get better for David, they got worse. Psalm 23 is the lament of human flesh wondering about his own death!

Lost in the house is a major theme, again picked up in the Luke passage of The Prodigal Son. But the younger son, who dared to leave home, spend his money, try his wild ventures, and come to himself to realize that a return trip home was necessary, is not the lost child that we assume. The older son, who did not venture out, do any risk-taking, or think outside of the box, ended up resentful, angry, and vindictive. He is the lost child! He never realized that he had everything because he was so busy looking at what his sibling received. The story ends without resolution. The question stands. How many lost children are in your pews?

Call to Worship

Leader: The God of those who are rejected, forgotten, and cast out comes seeking to receive, console, and heal.
People: We have come seeking The Good Shepherd.
Leader: The God of those who are wandering, wondering, and filled with anxious questions has come to answer questions, shower peace, and bring a stillness to raging storms.
People: We have come to meet with the Ultimate Answer.
Leader: The God of those who have left the safety of God's House, and the God of those who are lost in God's House, will find welcome here.
People: This day we worship, surrounded by Goodness and Mercy.
Thanks be to Almighty God!

Musical Suggestions for The Fourth Sunday of Lent

Hymns for the Day

Title	AAHH	AME	AMEZ	LEVS	LMGM	YL	HG
Come Ye Sinners, Poor and Needy	361	232	403	•	•	•	•
He Leadeth Me	142	395	292	•	•	391	•
How Great Thou Art	148	68	47	60	181	39	•
Love Divine, All Loves Excelling	440	455	274	•	•	38	•
O For a Thousand Tongues to Sing (AZMON)	184	1	21	•	•	1	•
O Love that Wilt Not Let Me Go	•	302	279	•	•	•	•
Savior, Like a Shepherd Lead Us	424	379	278	•	47	385	•
Softly and Tenderly	347	261	413	101	175	282	•
The Lord Is My Shepherd	426	206	74	104	152	•	•

Gospel Selections	AAHH	AME	AMEZ	LEVS	LMGM	YL	HG
Lead Me, Guide Me	474	378	•	194	168	•	•
Something Beautiful	•	•	269	•	•	472	•
Tell Jesus All	•	•	•	•	176	309	•
The Windows of Heaven	234	•	•	•	•	•	•

Anthems

The King of Love My Shepherd Is *Harry Rowe Shelley*
My Shepherd Will Supply My Need *John M. Rasley*
The Lord Is My Shepherd *Allen Pote*
My Shepherd Will Supply My Need *Virgil Thomson*
The Lord Is My Shepherd *Noble Cain*

Spirituals

King Jesus is A-Listening *William L. Dawson*
In His Care-O *Willima L. Dawson*
Jesus is a Rock in a Weary Land *Glenn Burleigh*

Gospel Selections

The Good Shepherd *V. Michael McKay*

Organ Music

A Lenten Suite *Charles Callahan*
Rhosymedre (or "Lovely") *Ralph Vaughan Williams*
The King of Love My Shepherd Is *David Cherwien* (from *Interpretations, Book III*)
The Lord's My Shepherd *David Cherwien* (from *Interpretations, Book III*)

The Fifth Sunday In Lent

Appropriate Banner and Altar Colors: Purple
Year A: Ezekiel 37: 1-14/ Psalm 130/Romans 8: 6-11/ John 11: 1-45
Year B: Jeremiah 31: 31-34/ Psalm 51: 1-12/ Hebrews 5: 5-10/ John 12: 20-33
Year C: Isaiah 43: 16-21/ Psalm 126/ Philippians 3: 4-14/ John 12: 1-8

Focus

To the vision of the dry bones in Ezekiel, the prophet answers God's question of "Can these bones live?" with the statement, "Lord, only you know." The answer shows up in Jesus, who walks into the graveyard where Lazarus has been for three days with sisters Mary and Martha. He announces to the grieving crowd, "I am the resurrection and the life, whoever believes in me shall never die." With a shout of, "Lazarus, come forward!" dry bones come shuttling forth, wrapped in stinking clothes. Jesus did not touch Lazarus. He commanded those standing there weeping, "Loose him and let him go!" What are the stinking clothes that we have "loosed" during this Lenten journey? Or, what's that smell in the sanctuary? The grateful dead was alive! The party was on as Death shivered in the face of Life Forevermore.

Sister Mary is a key figure this week, and she must not be overlooked! Mary was the High Priest who anointed Jesus in a foreigners home, outside of Jerusalem. She was the only believer in the house. While her sister stayed in a woman's assigned place fixing food, it was Mary the disciple who brought her own burial oil, approached The Master in the midst of hateful male talk, and poured the symbol of The Holy Spirit upon his head and washed his feet with her tears. Jesus said, "Wherever the Gospel is preached in the whole world, what she has done will be done in memory of her." (Matthew 26: 13) Read it and preach!

Call to Worship

>**Leader:** Let's shake, rattle and roll!
>**People:** How dare you talk to us like that?
>**Leader:** Without the Refreshing Spirit of God, we are simply a valley of very dry bones.
>**People:** Can we really be made alive? We do know that our bones are dried up, our hope is failing, and sometimes we do feel cut off from God.
>**Leader:** The Wind of Renewal speaks, "I will put my Spirit with you, you shall live, and I will give you your own place of security."
>**People:** The Life of the Universe has promised and will act on our behalf! We will offer praise unto our God!
(Trumpet A)

Musical Suggestions for The Fifth Sunday of Lent

Hymns for the Day

Title	AAHH	AME	AMEZ	LEVS	LMGM	YL	HG
Come Ye Sinners, Poor and Needy	361	232	403	•	•	•	•
I Lay My Sins on Jesus	•	•	426	•	•	•	•
Jesus Has Conquered Death		•	•	•	62	•	•
Lord, I'm Coming Home	•	260	559	•	•	316	•
Martha, Mary, Waiting, Weeping	•	•	•	•	•	•	102

Spirituals	AAHH	AME	AMEZ	LEVS	LMGM	YL	HG
Guide My Feet	131	386	•	•	•	•	•
Lord, I Want to Be a Christian	463	282	606	138	119	277	•
There Is a Balm in Gilead	524	425	619	203	157	119	•

Gospel Selections	AAHH	AME	AMEZ	LEVS	LMGM	YL	HG
Anointing	318	•	•	•	•	•	•

Anthems

Concertato on "What Wondrous Love Is This" *Ed Nowak*

Spirituals

Them Bones *Noah Ryder*

Lazarus *arr. Robert Tanner*

Ezekiel Saw the Wheel *William Dawson*

Dry Bones *J. Rosamond Johnson*

There Is a Balm in Gilead *arr. William Dawson*

Organ Music

Arietta *Samuel Coleridge-Taylor*

Come, Ye Sinners, Poor and Needy
George Shearing

Elegy *Samuel Coleridge-Taylor*

Palm Sunday
The Sixth Sunday of Lent

Appropriate Banner and Altar Colors: Purple and Red

Year A, B, and C: Isaiah 50: 4-9/ Psalm 31: 9-16/ Philippians 2: 5-11/

Year A: Matthew 26: 14-7: 66

Year B: Mark 11: 1-11 or John 12: 12-16

Year C: Luke 22: 19: 28-40

Focus

Everybody loves a good parade! It's the little child in us that longs to see the clowns, watch the animals, and laugh at the antics performed to attract us. Parades are about entertainment and spectators. Parades are about fun and foolishness. For what good is a parade without balloons, popcorn, and hot dogs sold along the street?

There were many people at the Palm Sunday parade for Jesus. For everybody loves a good parade! Jesus had a need that day from the community. It's odd to see Jesus asking for things. The Jesus that we know is always supplying the needs of others. He's healing the sick, feeding the hungry, touching and opening blind eyes, tending to little children, and raising the dead. For Jesus is a man who will meet the need! However, for the Triumphal Entry, Jesus sent the disciples to get a colt. And for the institution of The Lord's Supper, Jesus needed an upper room.

The community supplied each need. They didn't know that what they offered would be so monumental. They had no idea that thousands of years later, we would still be talking about the things they offered. Never was there a minor conception of how big that little attic would become, or that the King of Glory would be riding on that borrowed animal. What do we have to offer to The One who came to save us? Or, are you just one who simply came to be in the crowd, at the parade?

Benediction

Leader: The parade of palms is finished.

People: Hosannas are silent. The crowds have walked away.

Leader: During this week, someone will betray The Savior.

People: Lord, is it I?

Leader: Go, following the footsteps of Jesus to Calvary. The keeping power of The Holy Spirit goes with you. This will be a holy week of suffering, tears, and pain. But it is ours to remember. Resurrection Sunday is on the way!

People: Thanks be to God! Hallelujah and Amen.

(Trumpet For Zion, B)

Musical Suggestions for The Sixth Sunday (Palm Sunday)

Hymns for the Day

Title	AAHH	AME	AMEZ	LEVS	LMGM	YL	HG
All Glory, Laud and Honor	226	129	133	•	30	•	•
Hosanna	224	•	•	•	•	•	•
Hosanna, Loud Hosanna	•	130	132	•	•	•	•
Lift Up Your Heads, Ye Mighty Gates	•	94	137	•	•	•	•
Majesty	171	•	246	•	•	•	•
O Thou, Eternal Christ of God	•	•	134	•	•	•	•
Ride On! Ride on in Majesty	•	•	135	•	•	236	•

Spirituals	AAHH	AME	AMEZ	LEVS	LMGM	YL	HG
Come Out the Wilderness	367	•	•	258	465	•	

Gospel Selections	AAHH	AME	AMEZ	LEVS	LMGM	YL	HG
Ride On, King Jesus	225	•	•	97	•	•	•

Anthems

The Palms *Faure*
The Way to Jerusalem *Harold Friedell*
Lift Up Your Heads *E. L. Ashford*
Lift Up Your Heads, O Ye Gates *William Mathias*

Spirituals

Ride On, Jesus *arr. Roland M. Carter*
Leaning On the Lord *arr. Roland M. Carter*
Ride On, King Jesus *arr. Moses Hogan*

Gospel Selections

Hosanna! Hosanna! *Glenn Burleigh* (From "Let God Arise") Op. 35

Organ Music

March Upon a Theme of Handel, Op. 15, No. 2 *Alexandre Guilmant*
Partita on "All Glory, Laud, and Honor" *Michael Burkhardt*
Hosanna, Loud Hosanna *David Cherwien* (from *Interpretations, Book IX*)
Hosanna, Loud Hosanna *L. Wayne Kerr* (from *Augsburg Organ Library–Lent*)
Processional *William Mathias*

Holy Week

HOLY WEEK

This period of walking with Jesus to Calvary is not a usual and customary tradition in African American congregations. However, this is a prime evangelistic opportunity to reach out to your surrounding community with a soup and salad lunch followed by a short meditative worship experience. There are unchurched, previously churched, and out-of-the-area churched people who need to spend a few moments as we march toward Holy Thursday, Good Friday, and Easter. The readings signal the significance of what was happening to Jesus and the disciples during this last week of their ministry together.

Instead of using the Psalms as a responsive reading, I have provided a litany based upon the travels of Jesus. Following the readings, it may be helpful to provide a few moments of silence for personal reflection and meditation.

This period of walking with Jesus to Calvary is one to engage those not usually involved in the "busy life" of the congregation. Pulling together men and women who are retired to prepare the soup and salad each day gives ample opportunity for community building. Another suggestion would be to have this type of worship during each week of Lent. You may be pleasantly surprised at who will show up to a noon worship experience. Offering plates should be placed at the rear of the sanctuary and simply mentioned after the benediction. What monies are received will offset the cost of food and kitchen supplies. A particular mission in your local community can become the focus of any "additional" funds received.

Target schools, businesses, doctors' offices, and the area within a six-block radius of your building to leave flyers announcing lunch and meditation with a "free will offering." If your mission's work area is already involved with a local outreach project, mention it in your publicity. Some people who attend no congregation will be glad to give to "charity." Your church gets the credit and earns "brownie points" for caring. Invite those who "brown bag" for lunch to come and share the worship time with others as we journey to Calvary. Make this a meaningful occasion for Christ to touch hearts!

(See *AA Heritage Hymnal* for Litanies)

Monday of Holy Week

Appropriate Banner and Altar Colors: Purple

Isaiah 42:1–9

Psalm 36:5–11

Hebrews 9:11–15

John 12:1–11

Call to Worship

Leader: Here is my servant, whom I uphold. My chosen, in whom my soul delights.

People: God's spirit is upon him. Jesus will bring forth justice to the nations.

Leader: He will not cry or lift up his voice or make it heard in the street.

People: A bruised reed he will not break, and a dimly burning wick he will not quench.

Leader: Jesus will not grow faint or be crushed.

People: He is preparing to establish justice in the earth. We walk with him this week.

Call to Confession

The steadfast love of our God extends to the heavens. God's faithfulness is beyond the clouds. Our confession allows us the ability to take refuge in the shadow of God's wings. Let us pray.

Confession

The blood of goats and heifers will not satisfy the sacrifice required for us. We thank you God, for the blood of Jesus Christ, who entered once and for all into the Holy Place. Forgive us our sin. In the name of Love we pray. Amen.

Responsive Reading

Leader: Monday is the day of Jesus Christ's anointing.

People: The grateful dead was present.

Leader: Lazarus had already experienced resurrection.

People: The ungrateful thief was present.

Leader: Judas had his eye on what could be stolen.

People: Jesus was present.

Leader: And a woman anointed him as King.

People: She poured the anointing oil on his head as on a high priest.

Leader: She knelt down and worshiped at his feet.

People: The fragrance of her expensive ointment filled the room.

Leader: Instead of using the ointment for her own burial, she poured it all on Jesus.

People: The poor were present. They are yet among us. Jesus noticed them.

Leader: Her anointing prepared Jesus for the cross that was ahead.

People: A great crowd was present watching the sights, but not worshiping.

Leader: We gather to worship. We will walk with Jesus during this week of holy days.

Silence for meditation and personal reflection

BENEDICTION

Leader: Christ is the mediator of a new covenant.

People: We have been called to a new inheritance because of the sacrifice of Jesus.

Leader: Go in peace! Amen.

MUSICAL SUGGESTIONS FOR MONDAY OF HOLY WEEK

HYMNS FOR THE DAY

Title	AAHH	AME	AMEZ	LEVS	LMGM	YL	HG
He Understands, He'll Say "Well Done"	413	487	557	190	144	120	•
My Jesus, I Love Thee	574	457	•	89	35	335	•
Thy Way, O Lord	444	311	•	•	39	•	•
The Glory of these Forty Days	•	•	•	•	32	•	•
In the Bulb there Is a Flower	•	•	•	•	•	•	40
Lead Me to Calvary	253	306	•	31	•	317	•

Spirituals	AAHH	AME	AMEZ	LEVS	LMGM	YL	HG
Somebody's Knockin' at Your Door	348	•	•	100	34	•	•
Hush! Somebody's Callin' My Name	556	•	•	128	262	•	•

ANTHEMS

Isaac Watts Contemplates the Cross (Choral Cycle) *John W. Work, III*

1. When I Survey the Wondrous Cross
2. Alas, and Did My Savior Bleed
3. T'was on that Dark, Doleful Night
4. How Condescending and How Kind
5. Now for a Tune of Lofty Praise
6. Hosanna to the Prince of Light

SPIRITUALS

Here's One *William Grant Still*

(no. 6 in *The Oxford Book of Spirituals*, pp. 46-52)

GOSPEL SELECTIONS

See Appendix of Resources, # 8 *Born to Die*, pp. 140, and # 10 *Let God Arise*, pp. 141–142.

ORGAN MUSIC

Melody *Samuel Coleridge-Taylor*

Go to Dark Gethesmane *David Cherwien* (from *Augsburg Organ Library–Lent*)

Tuesday of Holy Week

Appropriate Banner and Altar Colors: Purple

Isaiah 49:1–7

Psalm 71

1 Corinthians 1:18–31

John 12:20–36

Call to Worship

Leader: Why have you gathered?

People: We want to see Jesus!

Leader: The Light is with us for only a little longer.

People: We will walk in the light.

Call to Confession

On this second day of Holy Week, as we walk toward Calvary, let us confess before God.

Confession

Loving God, the message of the cross is foolishness to those who are perishing, but to those of us who are being saved, it is the power of God. Forgive us our sin. Fill us with the power to follow you.

Words of Assurance

God is never far from us. The words of our confession draw us closer to the heart of God. This is good news.

Responsive Reading

Leader: The hour is coming closer. The appointed time is near.

People: Unless a grain of wheat falls to the earth and dies, it remains just a single grain.

Leader: But if it dies, it bears much fruit.

People: Those who love their life lose it. And those who hate their life in this world will keep it for eternal life.

Leader: Whoever serves Jesus must follow. For where Jesus goes, we must go also.

People: Now my soul is troubled! And what should we say?

Leader: It was for this reason that Jesus was born to die.

People: God will get the glory.

Leader: And the world will be judged.

People: The ruler of this world will be driven out.

Leader: And Jesus will be lifted up for all the world to see.

People: We walk with Jesus to Calvary.

Silence for meditation and personal reflection

Benediction

Leader: If you walk in the darkness, you do not know where you are going.

People: We leave to walk in the light. We are children of light.

Leader: The Light is with you a little longer. Go in peace!

Musical Suggestions for Tuesday of Holy Week

Hymns for the Day

Title	AAHH	AME	AMEZ	LEVS	LMGM	YL	HG
Before the Fruit Is Ripened	•	•	•	•	•	•	147
I Heard the Voice of Jesus (DRINK TO ME)	•	249	•	•	41	84	•
I Heard the Voice of Jesus (TRUMAN)	•	•	423	•	•	•	•
I Heard the Voice of Jesus (VOX DILECTI)	•	•	422	•	•	•	•
No, Not One	308	381	258	90	273	221	•
Lead Me to Calvary	253	306	•	31	•	317	•

Spirituals	AAHH	AME	AMEZ	LEVS	LMGM	YL	HG
Give Me Jesus	561	•	•	91	280	•	•

Gospel Selections	AAHH	AME	AMEZ	LEVS	LMGM	YL	HG
Jesus, I Love You	•	•	•	•	268	•	•
My Soul Loves Jesus	581	•	•	•	245	82	•

Anthems

(See Monday of Holy Week)

Gospel Selections

See Appendix of Resources, # 8 *Born to Die*, pp. 140, and # 10 *Let God Arise*, pp. 141–142.

Organ Music

Go to Dark Gethsemane *David Cherwien* (from *Augsburg Organ Library–Lent*)

Of the Glorious Body Telling *Ronald Arnatt* (from *Augsbury Organ Library–Lent*)

Wednesday of Holy Week

Appropriate Banner and Altar Colors: Purple

Isaiah 50:4–9

Psalm 70

Hebrews 12:1–3

John 13:21–32

Call to Worship

Leader: God has given us tongues that we might teach others.

People: God calls us to sustain the weary with our meager words.

Leader: Morning by morning God gives us alert ears.

People: God has opened our ears so we may be taught.

Leader: When we do not rebel and turn from God, we will be used in ministry to the world.

People: Let us stand up together. The Lord, our God, is our constant help.

Call to Confession

God is pleased to deliver us. We only need to ask forgiveness for our sin.

Confession

Gracious God, we have been rebellious and turned away from you. We have fallen into sin and brought disgrace to our witness. Forgive us our sin. Deliver us. Set our face like flint so that we might see no evil, hear no evil, and do no evil in your sight. Declare us "not guilty" in order that we may serve you in the world.

Words of Assurance

Therefore, since we are surrounded by so great a cloud of witnesses, let us also lay aside every weight and the sin that clings so closely. Let us run with perseverance the race that is set before us looking to Jesus, the pioneer and perfecter of our faith, who for the sake of the joy that was set before him endured the cross, disregarding its shame, and has taken his seat at the right hand of the throne of God. Consider him, who endured such hostility against himself from sinners, so that you may not grow weary or lose heart. My sisters and brothers, this is certainly good news!

Responsive Reading

Leader: The Teacher became a mother one night.

People: Jesus prepared his children a meal. He used his own body and his own blood.

Leader: The Great One became a mother one night.

People: Jesus prepared his children a bath and washed their dirty feet.

Leader: The Parent became sad one night.

People: After preparing and serving, washing and wishing, he knew betrayal was close at hand.

Leader: Jesus said, "Very truly, I tell you, one of you will betray me."

People: John asked, "Lord, who is it?"

Leader: That question continues to ring loud among us today.

People: We ask, "Lord, is it me?"

Silence for meditation and personal reflection

BENEDICTION

Leader: We are walking with Jesus to Calvary.

People: Who among us will betray the Sovereign of Creation?

Leader: Go in peace!

MUSICAL SUGGESTIONS FOR WEDNESDAY OF HOLY WEEK

HYMNS FOR THE DAY

Title	AAHH	AME	AMEZ	LEVS	LMGM	YL	HG
I Must Tell Jesus	375	388	526	66	267	74	•
Jesus, Remember Me	230	•	•	•	48	•	•
Lord, Help Us Walk Your Servant Way	•	•	•	•	•	•	150
Lead Me to Calvary	253	306	•	31	•	317	•

Gospel Selections	AAHH	AME	AMEZ	LEVS	LMGM	YL	HG
I Love Him	236	•	•	•	44	125	•
I Love the Lord	395	313	•	67	238	53	•
Jesus, You Brought Me All the Way	•	•	•	•	253	•	•

ANTHEMS

(See Monday of Holy Week)

SPIRITUALS

When I Was Sinking Down *Hall Johnson*

GOSPEL SELECTIONS

See Appendix of Resources, # 8 *Born to Die*, pp. 140, and # 10 *Let God Arise*, pp. 141–142.

ORGAN MUSIC

Ah, Jesus Dear, Op. 122, No. 2 *Johannes Brahms*

Ah, Holy Jesus *Beverly A. Ward* (from *Augsburg Organ Music–Lent*)

My Song is Love Unknown *Ralph Vaughan Williams* (from *Augsburg Organ Library–Lent*)

Calvary *Richard Billingham* (from *Seven Reflections on African American Spirituals*)

Holy Thursday

In the black Church, this night has been deemed appropriate for the washing of feet. It is an old custom that seems to have lost its appeal in recent generations. Yet the Savior washed the feet of his disciples on this sacred night. And we can return to this tradition, which indicates humility and service to another. If feet washing is not desired, some sort of hand washing ritual may be exchanged, with lotion provided to conclude our act of care. It is also the night that the Passover Meal is celebrated. This meal is the one eaten just before the children of Israel began their exodus from slavery in Egypt. As they were to be busy packing up and preparing for the signal to move out, the meal was to be eaten while the participants were on alert. On this night, Holy Thursday, the congregation could be asked to pack the typical meal that our ancestors might have packed as they were preparing for moving out under the cover of night for freedom. Brought in picnic baskets, this meal is a prime opportunity to celebrate together and to covenant anew to be community for each other.

Call to Worship
Read Exodus 12: 1–14.

Song of Celebration *(see Hymns for the Day)*

Call to Sharing a Meal

The feast of the slave community has always held a special place in our hearts. We can easily remember Granny packing the basket as we made ready to travel to worship, to a quilting bee, or simply to spend time with our kin. As we migrated from the south to the north and Midwest, we can recall with fondness the many brown bags, packed with fried chicken, homemade rolls, deviled eggs, fried pies, and potato salad that traveled with us, in trains, buses, and cars. These meals sustained us in times that the dining cars didn't welcome us. Eating together has been part of our salvation. The Jewish community has its meal, which Jesus celebrated with his friends. In that same spirit, tonight we will open our picnic baskets around the tables and share with our friends. Freedom is on the way. Let's be ready to heed its call.

Table Grace

God, you continue to call us to make haste for freedom. We thank you for your call. As we gather around these tables in celebration of the awesome ministry of Jesus to and with his friends, help us to remember his servant attitude. He prepared and served a meal. He washed the feet of his friends and affirmed them. Help us to follow his example on this holy night. Bless the abundance of food that has been prepared and that we will eat. Bless each hand that touched it in order for it to grace our tables. Bless those folks with little and those with none tonight. Bless those folks who are yet willingly shackled in bondage. Sanctify this food as nourishment for our bodies. And when we leave this place, let its nutrition energize us enough to work towards the day when the world can gather around banquet tables like these with thanksgiving. In the name of Jesus Christ we pray. Amen.

After Supper Response

Congregational song of praise

Scripture Reading

Read John 13: 1–7, 31b–35

Invitation to Servanthood

Love is an action verb. Our foreparents washed each other's feet as a sign of love, care, and service. Tonight we will offer a similar sign by washing each other's hands. Handiwipes are available at each table. After each one has cleaned another's hand, let us take the time to put lotion on that same pair of hands. Then let us pray for the ministry opportunities before our neighbors.

Hymn of Praise

(see Hymns for the Day)

Call to Communion

1 Corinthians 11: 23–26

Communion is served.

Benediction

(Read responsively Psalm 116:1–2, 12–19)

Leader: Go in peace to love God and to serve your neighbors in all that you do.

People: Amen and amen.

Musical Suggestions for Holy Thursday

Hymns for the Day

Title	AAHH	AME	AMEZ	LEVS	LMGM	YL	HG
Fasting with My Lord	•	•	•	•	•	60	•
Jesu, Jesu, Fill Us with Your Love	•	•	•	•	33	•	•
One Bread, One Body	•	•	•	151	139	•	•
Wash, O God, Our Sons and Daughters	674	•	•	•	•	•	•

Spirituals	AAHH	AME	AMEZ	LEVS	LMGM	YL	HG
Let Us Break Bread Together	686	530	338	152	135	30	•

Gospel Selections	AAHH	AME	AMEZ	LEVS	LMGM	YL	HG
This Do In Remembrance	•	532	•	•	•	•	•
Koinonia	579	•	•	•	•	•	•
Lord, I Have Seen Thy Salvation	679	•	•	153	•	•	•

Anthems

With a Voice of Singing *Martin Shaw*

Drop, Drop, Slow Tears *Charles Callahan*

Go to Dark Gethsemane *T. Tertius Noble*

This is My Body, This is My Blood *John A. Behnke*

Spirituals

Let Us Break Bread Together *arr. William Lawrence* (no. 7 in *The Oxford Book of Spirituals*, pp. 53-56)

Let Us Break Bread Together *arr. Noah Ryder*

Gospel Selections

This Do in Remembrance of Me *Glenn Burleigh*

Sacramentum *V. Michael McKay*

Do This In Mem'ry of Me *James B. Kinchen, Jr.*

Organ Music

May Be duh Las' Time, Ah Don' Know! *William Farley Smith* (from *Songs of Deliverance*)

Deep River *William Farley Smith* (from *Songs of Deliverance*)

Steal Away *Raymond Haan*

Prelude on "Drop, Drop, Slow Tears" *Vincent Persichetti*

Good Friday

This worship experience is an alternative to the preaching style commonly used. This can be a worship of scripture and songs appropriate to the Word Jesus speaks. It is a time when lay speakers, young and senior, can participate in meaningful ways.

The sanctuary is dark as the congregation gathers. Acolytes enter and light altar candles. The processional of the male choir is next, followed by their acapella singing of an appropriate spiritual. When they are finished and seated, the spotlight follows Jesus and Simon, slowly coming up the aisle bearing the cross. It is laid against pulpit where it is very visible.

Appropriate Banner and Altar Colors: Red

Call to Worship

(Isaiah 52:13–53:12)

Jesus and Simon leave as congregation stands to sing. *(Music selected by musicians)*

Invocation

On this most sacred night, we gather to remember. We remember the greatest sacrifice of love. We remember the journey of Jesus to the cross. We remember the price Jesus paid for our salvation. And we remember our sinfulness. We remember that his disciples ran away afraid. We remember that Jesus was left alone. Tonight, we gather to be present. Gracious God, this night, we gather to remember. Thank you for Jesus. Thank you for your presence. Thank you for your love. Thank you for this holy memory. For the sake of Jesus Christ we pray. Amen.

Scripture

Hebrews 10: 16–25

Congregational Hymn

The Seven Last Words of Jesus

The First Word (Luke 23: 26–38) *Father Forgive Them*, Solo

The Second Word (Luke 23: 39–43) *Today You Are With Me*

Congregational Hymn

The Third Word (John 19: 25–27) *Woman, Behold Thy Son*

The Fourth Word (John 19: 28) *I Thirst*

Congregational Hymn

The Fifth Word (Psalm 22) *My God, My God, Why?* Solo

The Sixth Word (Luke 23:44–46) *Into Thy Hands*

The Seventh Word (John 19:29–30) *It Is Finished!*

The pastor invites all musical participants to the altar. Each one is given a nail for the cross. Sound effects, offstage, enlarge the sound of pounding. The pastor invites the congregation to the altar as ushers hand out nails to take home to remember this significant night. (Congregation can bring offering forward as they come to kneel and pray.) When the last person leaves the altar, the music ceases. When all have finished, the communion stewards silently strip the altar. The lights are turned off with the exception of a spotlight on the cross. There is a space of silence. The pastor instructs the congregation to leave in thanksgiving and silence. There is no additional music or talking.

Musical Suggestions for Good Friday

Hymns for the Day

Title	AAHH	AME	AMEZ	LEVS	LMGM	YL	HG
He Will Remember Me	240	475	•	34	36	117	•
I See a Crimson Stream	268	•	•	•	•	•	•
O Sacred Head Sore Wounded	250	133	172	36	•	•	•
The Old Rugged Cross	244	144	157	38	37	246	•
There Is a Fountain Filled with Blood	257	255	342	39	•	249	•

Spirituals	AAHH	AME	AMEZ	LEVS	LMGM	YL	HG
Calvary	239	•	•	32	38	•	•
He Never Said a Mumblin' Word	•	•	155	33	•	251	•
I Know It Was the Blood	267	•	•	•	•	253	•
Were You There?	254	136	156	37	43	260	•

Gospel Selections	AAHH	AME	AMEZ	LEVS	LMGM	YL	HG
Oh, the Blood of Jesus	265	•	•	•	•	•	•
Remember Me	434	•	•	179	209	•	•

Anthems

There Is a Fountain Filled With Blood
   arr. Wendell P. Whalum

From Bethlehem to Calvary   *Jonathan Varcoe*
Crucifixion (He Never Said a Mumblin' Word)
   Adolphus Hailstork

Spirituals

Were You There   *arr. Norman Luboff*
   (no. 16 in *The Oxford Book of Spirituals*, pp. 130-135)
Everytime I Think About Jesus   *arr. L. L. Fleming*

Look What Dey Doin' to Jesus   *arr. Richard Jackson*
   (no. 26 in *The Oxford Book of Spirituals*, pp. 213-221)
Oh, That Bleeding Lamb   *Undine Smith Moore*

Gospel Selections

He Decided to Die   *Margaret Douroux*

Oh the Blood   *Carlton Burgess*

Organ Music

Passacaglia   *David Hurd* (*Anthology of African American Organ Music*, Vol. 4)
Were You There?   *David Hurd* (from *Four Spiritual Preludes*)
Were You There?   *Leo Sowerby*
Meditation on 'Were You There?'   *Evelyn Simpson-Curenton* (*Anthology of African American Organ Music*, Vol. 3)
Solemn Processional   *Robert A. Harris* (*Anthology of African American Organ Music*, Vol. 2)

Holy Saturday

Appropriate Banner and Altar Colors: White

Call to Worship

Leader: Each of us is born.
People: Our days are too short and filled with trouble.
Leader: We come up like a flower and we wither.
People: Like a fleeting shadow we do not last.
Leader: Our days are determined.
People: Our death is certain.
Leader: Yesterday, death claimed Jesus!
People: A funeral procession followed his body to a borrowed tomb.
Leader: It is not the end of the story.
People: Thanks be to God.

Call to Confession

Mortals die. Jesus died. He was ready, prepared, and able to say, "It is finished!" Our confession helps us to stay prepared to meet death. Let us pray.

Confession

In you, O God, we seek refuge; do not let us ever be put to shame. Forgive our sin. In your righteousness, deliver us from the bonds of death. Incline your ears to us. Rescue speedily. Be our rock of refuge and our strong fortress of salvation. Our times are in your hand. In the name of the Savior we pray.

Words of Assurance

God's face shines upon us when we confess our sin. It is with steadfast love that we are forgiven and made whole. This is good news.

Responsive Reading

Leader: A wealthy but secret disciple, Joseph of Arimathea, received the body of Jesus for burial.
People: Lord, where were your vocal followers?
Leader: Pilate allowed a secret disciple to take the wrapped body of a dead Jesus and lay it in a borrowed tomb.
People: Lord, where were your vocal followers?
Leader: A great stone was rolled in front of the door to seal the tomb. The funeral procession was very small. There were three women and one man, a disciple, at the funeral.
People: Lord, where were your vocal followers?
Leader: The chief priests and the Pharisees gathered before Pilate to plot.
People: Lord, where were your vocal followers?
Leader: They decided to put guards all around the tomb to keep Jesus locked inside a grave.
People: Lord, where were your vocal followers?
Leader: The women followers sat silent, opposite the tomb, preparing to do their last act of loving ministry to a dead corpse at the proper time.
People: Jesus died. His followers did not remember his words of assurance that he would rise. Today the whole world waits as Jesus lies in a tomb.
Leader: Lord, where are your vocal followers? (All of Holy Week: Trumpet B)

Musical Suggestions for Holy Saturday

Hymns for the Day

Title	AAHH	AME	AMEZ	LEVS	LMGM	YL	HG
He Will Remember Me	240	475	•	34	36	117	•
I See a Crimson Stream	268	•	•	•	•	•	•
O Sacred Head Sore Wounded	250	133	172	36	•	•	•
The Old Rugged Cross	244	144	157	38	37	246	•
There Is a Fountain Filled with Blood	257	255	342	39	•	249	•

Spirituals	AAHH	AME	AMEZ	LEVS	LMGM	YL	HG
Calvary	239	•	•	32	38	•	•
He Never Said a Mumblin' Word	•	•	155	33	•	251	•
I Know It Was the Blood	267	•	•	•	•	253	•
Were You There?	254	136	156	37	43	260	•

Gospel Selections	AAHH	AME	AMEZ	LEVS	LMGM	YL	HG
Oh, the Blood of Jesus	265	•	•	•	•	•	•
Remember Me	434	•	•	179	209	•	•

Anthems

There Is a Fountain Filled With Blood *arr. Wendell P. Whalum* (MAR-VEL)

From Bethlehem to Calvary *Jonathan Varcoe*

Spirituals

Were You There *arr. Norman Luboff*
   (no. 16 in *The Oxford Book of Spirituals*, pp. 130-135)

Everytime I Think About Jesus *arr. L. L. Fleming*

Look What Dey Doin' to Jesus *arr. Richard Jackson*
   (no. 26 in *The Oxford Book of Spirituals*, pp. 213-221)

Gospel Selections

He Decided to Die *Margaret Douroux*

Oh the Blood *Carlton Burgess*

Precious Blood of Jesus *arr. Joseph Joubert*

Organ Music

Passacaglia *David Hurd* (*Anthology of African American Organ Music* Vol. 4)

Were You There? *David Hurd* (from *Four Spiritual Preludes*)

Were You There? *Leo Sowerby*

Meditation on 'Were You There?' *Evelyn Simpson-Curenton*
   (*Anthology of African American Organ Music*, Vol. 3)

Solemn Processional *Robert A. Harris* (*Anthology of African American Organ Music*, Vol. 2)

Bye and Bye *William Farley Smith* (from *Songs of Deliverance*)

O Sacred Head Now Wounded *arr. Michael Burkhardt* (from *Five Lenten Hymn Improvisations*)

EASTERTIDE

THE EASTER SEASON

The resurrection is about our ability to rise! Jesus was tormented, mocked, caused public shame, and ultimately killed. Evil felt it had the final word. Death considered itself a victor. The grave thought itself "the end." But Jesus got up! Evil's chain was broken and death's hold was denied. The grave was forced to release its captive. God's power was evidenced as Jesus, the Christ, rose from the grave. The resurrection is about our ability to be like Jesus Christ and to rise! We rise above evil circumstances. We rise above the death of hopes and dreams. We rise above our graves of depression, desolation, and despair. Every Sunday's worship experience is another celebration of the resurrection. Getting up and beginning again is our theme song of joyous and unending praise.

Easter Sunday

Appropriate Banner and Altar Colors: White

Year A, B, and C: Acts 10: 34-43/Psalm 118: 1-2, 14-24/ 1 Corinthians 15: 1-11

Year A: John 20: 1-18

Year B: Mark 16: 1-8

Year C: Luke 24: 1-12

Focus

Every Gospel story points to women on a journey to do ministry to a corpse. This was the work of women. Not only did they birth and bath the infants, but they did the ministry of "embalming" the bodies with perfumed oils and wrapped them in cloths for burial as well. These were the women who loved Jesus and had watched his cruel death. These were the women who sat with his mother on the night after his crucifixion and wept in grief. These were the women who were concerned about their lack of physical strength to move the stone grave enclosure, yet continued on their journey to the grave. These were the women who found the stone already gone! These were the women who first encountered resurrection. Too often we refuse to move ahead for fear of the size of "the stone." What happens to our excuses when "the stone" is moved for us?

It was a woman, Mary Magdelene, who searched in the garden as she wept. It was a woman with a bad reputation who went and told the male disciples that the grave was empty. It was this same woman who stayed in the garden, continuing her diligent search for the body, after the disciples returned to their "hiding" place. And it was this woman who had a conversation with the one she "supposed" was a gardener and heard her name called and then recognized Jesus, The Christ! It was this woman, Mary Magdelene, to whom the first message of the resurrection was given. This was a "new garden" experience. Mary Magdelene enacted the role of Eve. Jesus was the second Adam. Could this possibly have been a liberation event for women in the Church?

Call to Worship

Leader: Christ the Lord is risen!

People: Christ the Lord is risen indeed!

Leader: We celebrate the Lord of Life!

People: We give praise to the God who conquered death.

Leader: We bless the Lord who took the victory away from hell.

People: We worship the Lord who won for us eternal life!

Leader: We have a story to tell.

People: New life begins again. Christ the Lord is risen indeed!

Call to Confession

God shows no partiality, but anyone who shows reverence and does what is right is acceptable. With our confession, we join The Lord of Life.

Confession

God, the message of Jesus has spread, beginning in Galilee. With the power of The Holy Spirit, Jesus went about doing good and healing all who were oppressed by evil. Too often we have participated in the oppression of powerlessness and we have refused to do the good that we know. Forgive us our sin. Grant us new life, we pray in the name of he who rose victorious from the dead.

Words of Assurance

All the prophets testify about him that everyone who believes in Jesus Christ receives forgiveness of sins through his name. This is our salvation. Thanks be to God.

Responsive Reading

Leader: God has done it again!

People: It's been a long journey to new life.

Leader: But God has done it again!

People: Fridays are deadly, but the day of resurrection does come!

Leader: God has done it again!

People: For every closed eye is not sleeping, and every good-bye ain't gone!

Leader: God has done it again!

People: For evil thought Jesus was down and out, but death was only a comma, not God's period!

Leader: God has done it again!

People: We are an Easter People, and rising is always our theme of praise.

Leader: God has done it again!

People: The impossible has been made possible. The unthinkable is visible.

Leader: God has done it again!

People: We shall not die, but we shall live and give glory to God with our deeds.

Leader: God has done it again!

People: The gates of righteousness have been opened for us.

Leader: God has done it again!

People: The stone that the builders rejected has become the chief cornerstone.

Leader: This is the Lord's doing and it's marvelous in our eyes. This is the day the Lord has made. We will rejoice and be glad in it.

People: For God has done it again!

Offertory Invitation

We have been handed down that which we have received. Christ died for our sin in accordance with the scriptures, and was buried and was raised on the third day. This news is worth our sharing. Our gifts will keep the message spreading to new generations.

Offertory Praise

God, it is by your amazing grace that we are what we are today. Your grace toward us has not been in vain. We recognize that it was not of our own capabilities, but your divine ability to pursue us that brought us unto you. Our gifts are simply a meager attempt to say thanks. We offer them in the Name of Love.

Benediction

Leader: Leave with a message upon your lips.

People: I have seen the Lord.

Leader: Leave with a message upon your hearts.

People: I have seen the Lord.

Leader: Leave with a message being your life.

People: I have seen the Lord.

Leader: He is risen!

People: Christ the Lord is risen indeed!

Leader: Go in that faith-filled power to love God and to serve your neighbor in all that you do!

People: Hallelujah and Amen. (Trumpet B)

Musical Suggestions for Easter Sunday

Hymns for the Day

Title	AAHH	AME	AMEZ	LEVS	LMGM	YL	HG
Christ Arose	283	•	184	•	•	261	•
Christ Has Arisen	•	•	•	41	61	•	•
Christ the Lord Is Risen Today	282	156	176	•	57	263	•
He Lives	275	•	187	42	•	•	•
He Rose Triumphantly	•	•	•	•	•	262	•
I Know that My Redeemer Lives (DUKE STREET)	276	•	•	•	63	•	•
Jesus Christ Is Risen Today (EASTER HYMN)	•	•	•	•	58	•	•
Jesus Christ Is Risen Today (LLANFAIR)	•	161	195	•	•	•	•
The Strife Is O'er	277	162	181	•	64	•	•

Spirituals	AAHH	AME	AMEZ	LEVS	LMGM	YL	HG
Amen	649	172	•	233	•	•	•
Go and Tell Mary and Martha	284	•	•	•	•	•	•
He Arose	280	170	•	40	59	•	•
The Angel Rolled the Stone Away	279	•	•	•	•	•	•

Gospel Selections	AAHH	AME	AMEZ	LEVS	LMGM	YL	HG
Because He Lives	281	•	193	43	•	265	•
Hallelujah to the Risen Lamb	278	•	•	•	•	•	•

ANTHEMS

Hallelujah from "Mount of Olives" *Beethoven*

Easter Antiphon *David Hurd*

Alleluia *Charles Coleman*

Processional for Easter (Christ Our Passover) *David Hurd*

Worthy Is the Lamb/Amen from "Messiah" *Handel*

The Day of Resurrection *Thomas Matthews*

Hallelujah! *William D. Brown*

Hallelujah Chorus from "Messiah" *G. F. Handel* #264 YL

SPIRITUALS

Amen arr. *Jester Harriston*
   (no. 14 in *The Oxford Book of Spirituals*)

GOSPEL SELECTIONS

He Has the Power *Leon Roberts*

Resurrection Day *V. Michael McKay*

No Greater Love *David L. Allen*

He Got Up *V. Michael McKay*

ORGAN MUSIC

Toccata on "Christ the Lord Is Risen Today" *arr. Diane Bish*

O, de Angels Roll'd duh Stone Away *William Farley Smith* (from *Songs of Deliverance*)

Toccata *Mark Fax* (from *Three Organ Pieces*)

Alleluyas *Simon Preston*

Up from the Grave He Arose *John Ferguson* (from *Augsburg Organ Library–Easter*)

Toccata (from *Symphony No. 5*) *Charles M. Widor*

The Second Sunday of Easter

Appropriate Banner and Altar Colors: White

Year A: Acts 2: 14, 22-32, Psalm 16, 1 Peter 1: 3-9, John 20: 19-31

Year B: Acts 4: 32-35/ Psalm 133/ 1 John 1: 1-2:2/ John 20: 19-31

Year C: Acts 5: 27-32/ Psalm 118: 14-29/ Revelation 1: 4-8/ John 20: 19-31

Focus

The scared, frightened, and anxious disciples were yet in hiding. Those who had run away, left the Teacher, and been absent at both the Cross and the grave were sitting together, looking at each other and remembering the "good old days." They had lost their purpose. They had lost their fighting spirit. They had given up on their goal of catching souls! They were trying to figure out what to do next. They had heard that the body of Jesus was gone. They had heard that the grave was empty. They had heard that Mary Magdelene had spoken to someone who looked like Jesus. But they did not and could not believe. They had already forgotten his messages of victory. They felt like failures. They were hiding like cowards. They looked like a group of men who had lost their way. Then into the room appeared Jesus Christ!

At our worst point of failure, Jesus shows up. When we are feeling our lowest, Jesus arrives on the scene. When we have given up on our hopes, our dreams, and our visions of better days, that's when Jesus will appear. Jesus did not disturb the doors they had blocked for fear of the Roman soldiers. Jesus did not break one piece of glass on the covered windows. Jesus simply appeared before them. And when he begin to speak, it was not with harsh words of rebuke. When Jesus spoke to them, it was not with blame and shame. When he opened his mouth, "He taught them saying, Shalom!"

Jesus came to bring peace to their wounded souls and broken spirits. Jesus came to speak peace to the blame game that we have a tendency to start when life goes berserk! Jesus came and offered them the very last thing they expected: peace. Isn't this just like Jesus? Then he breathed on them the keeping power of The Holy Spirit to ensure that they remembered the precious gift he had bestowed. Hallelujah! What a Savior!

Leader: The Resurrecting God is present.

People: We have been dead in trespasses and sin.

Leader: The God of new life is here.

People: We are stormy weather people, seeking the Son!

Leader: God seeks those who believe that fresh starts belong to them.

People: With believing hearts, willing minds, and expectant spirits, we offer the God of Resurrection praise. (Trumpet A)

Visuals

Different types of locks, doves, and even a barred window would be appropriate altar symbols to address the gospel passages. A tall screen door with bars and a lock with a large bird atop is also appropriate. The Garden scene has been dismantled and the appearances of Jesus will change week by week. Overhead are scenes of blowing winds speaking to the gift of The Holy Spirit.

Musical Suggestions for The Second Sunday of Easter

Hymns for the Day

Title	AAHH	AME	AMEZ	LEVS	LMGM	YL	HG
Crown Him with Many Crowns	288	174	199	•	68	•	•
Lo, He Comes with Clouds Descending	•	99	•	•	•	•	•
The Day of Resurrection (LANCASHIRE)	•	159	•	•	•	•	•
The Day of Resurrection (ROTTERDAM)	•	160	•	•	•	•	•
Thine Is the Glory	•	157	194	•	•	•	•

Spirituals	AAHH	AME	AMEZ	LEVS	LMGM	YL	HG
Amen	649	172	•	233	•	•	•

Gospel Selections	AAHH	AME	AMEZ	LEVS	LMGM	YL	HG
He's So Real	237	•	•	•	227	489	•
This Is the Day the Lord Hath Made	108	•	42	219	•	•	•
Yes, God Is Real	162	361	53	209	226	128	•

Anthems

Alleluia *Ralph Manuel*
Lift High the Cross *arr. Todd Wilson*
Easter Hymn *Ralph Vaughan Williams*
A Song to the Lamb *Gerre Hancock*
An Alleluia Canon for Easter *David Hurd*
Antiphon - Let All the World in Every Corner Sing (from *Five Mystical Songs*) *Ralph Vaughan Williams*

Spirituals

Were You There? *Harry T. Burleigh*

Gospel Selections

Jesus Purchased My Salvation *Robert Fryson*
Redeemed *V. Michael McKay*
I Thank God for the Blood *V. Michael McKay*

Organ Music

I Know that My Redeemer Lives *George Shearing* (Sacred Music Press)
In Death's Strong Grasp the Savior Lay, BWV 625 *J. S. Bach* (Orgelbüchlein)
We Know That Christ is Raised *David Cherwien* (from *Augsburg Organ Library–Easter*)

Third Sunday of Easter

Appropriate Banner and Altar Colors: White
Year A: Acts 2: 36-41/ Psalm 116: 1-19/ 1 Peter 1: 17-23/ Luke 24: 13-35
Year B: Acts 3: 12-19/ Psalm 4/ 1 John 3: 1-7/ Luke 24: 36-48
Year C: Acts 9: 1-20/Psalm 30/ Revelation 5: 11-14/ John 21: 1-19

Focus

It is such a common thing until we take it for granted. It is such a part of our daily routine until we barely stop to think about how sacred an act we are participating in at the moment. We do it so often until we fail to recognize how meaningful the ritual was to Jesus until we come to these gospel passages of sharing food, breaking bread together, and having conversation around a meal. For in these gospel messages, Jesus is recognized as he offers to his followers what we now call the Lord's Supper. Their eating with him refreshed their memories.

This is one of those teachable moments when the risen Savior calls the disciples "children." This is one of those "a ha" moments, when they are sent back out after fishing all night and catching nothing, as they had done the very night he had first called them to the ministry of souls. This is an eye-opening moment when the disciple with the biggest mouth, who has denied Jesus three times, is asked three times, "Do you love me?" This is an "Oh, now I see" moment, when Jesus walks "a piece of the way" with two believers who ask him if he is the only one in the area who has not heard about the death of The Teacher! We all have these moments. Jesus makes appearance after appearance and is not recognized at first. Let's remember to always take a closer look!

Offertory Invitation

The Jesus question to the disciples after the resurrection was, "Do you have anything here to eat?" The disciples were caught off guard, and the reality helped them to see Jesus more clearly. It is not in what we have that we see Jesus. It is in what we share that others see the reality of The Risen Christ. Let us give with a spirit of generosity.

Offertory Praise

Jesus opened the minds of the disciples to understand the scriptures. Please accept these gifts as our comprehension that it is indeed far better to give than to receive. Bless both the gift and the givers we pray in the name of The Messiah.
(Trumpet B)

Visual Aids

In the middle of the altar, this is a good time to sit an African American rendition of Rodan's *The Thinker*. There are carvings of women and children who show us the reality of thinking, pondering, and meditating, which the disciples certainly had to do when they realized that they had not known the risen Teacher. Overheads of people eating at different functions assist us in remembering that whenever we sit at a meal with another, Christ is present in the breaking of our bread.

Musical Suggestions for The Third Sunday of Easter

Hymns for the Day

Title	AAHH	AME	AMEZ	LEVS	LMGM	YL	HG
Abide with Me	459	495	576	·	313	374	·
Amazing Grace	271	226	501	181	173	80	·
And Can It Be That I Should Gain	·	459	345	·	·	·	·
Let All That Is within Me Cry Holy	·	·	·	85	203	·	·
The Church's One Foundation	337	519	304	·	·	88	·
Thine Be the Glory	·	157	194	·	·	·	·

Anthems

The Church's One Foundation *arr. Roger Holland, III*
Amazing Grace *arr. Wendell P. Whalum*
God So Loved the World *Lanny Wolfe* AAHH
The Promise Which Was Made Unto the Fathers
   Edward Bairstow
Amazing Grace *arr. Evelyn Simpson-Curenton*
God So Loved the World *John Staine*
The Strife Is O'er *Paul Leddington Wright*

Spirituals

Let Us Break Bread Together *arr. Noah Ryder*

Gospel Selections

Sacramentum *V. Michael McKay*
I've Fall in Love with Jesus *V. Michael McKay*

Organ Music

God of Grace, Op. 14 *Paul Manz*
Chorale Prelude on "Eventide" *C. Hubert Parry*
Let Us Break Bread Together *Charles Callahan*
Toccata on "Amazing Grace" *J. Christopher Pardini*

Fourth Sunday of Easter

Appropriate Banner and Altar Colors: White
Year A: Acts 2: 42-47/ Psalm 23/ 1 Peter 2: 19-25/ John 10: 1-10
Year B: Acts 4: 5-12/ Psalm 23/ 1 John 3: 16-24/ John 10: 11-18
Year C: Acts 9: 36-43/ Psalm 23/ Revelation 7: 9-17/ John 10: 22-30

Focus

The Lamb of God, who takes away the sins of the world, is featured throughout the readings for this day. For only The Lamb is worthy to be the blood covering for all who confess him, regardless of race, nation, tribe, or tongue. Yet the Lamb is also The Great Shepherd of the sheep. Jesus depicts himself as the one who is willing to lay himself in front of the gate to keep the fold from any hurt or harm. He did it because of his great love. This love has been sacrificed for us. It is now our turn to pass the love along.

Tabitha's love is made evident in the many people she makes clothes for and offers herself to them in service. With her death, these grateful people come with tearful laments and testify to her following in the loving steps of Jesus. She, like Jesus, is raised from the dead. The "new" Church is showing love for each other in the acts of studying together, breaking bread together, and having prayer and fellowship together, as well as putting all their belongings into a common pot for the sake of community equality. Obedience to loving each other is a mark, symbol, and sign of the way The Good Shepherd brings many new members into "the fold!"

Visual Aids

A shepherd's crook or group of toy sheep will speak to the altar theme this day. An open Bible, with a crown over it, addresses the Book of Life theme. Overhead pictures of people ministering to the homeless, at shelters, and in soup lines are evidence of how we pass along Christ's love.

Responsive Reading

Leader: The Lord is my Shepherd. I shall not want.
People: This is our confidence.
Leader: He makes me lie down in green pastures.
People: This is our restoration.
Leader: He leadeth me besides the still waters. He restores my soul.
People: This is our healing.
Leader: He leads me in right paths for his name's sake.
People: This is our direction and security.
Leader: Even though I walk through the valley of death, I fear no evil. You are with me.
People: This is our faith.
Leader: Your rod and your staff comfort me.
People: This is our blessed assurance.
Leader: You prepare a table before me in the presence of my enemies.
People: This is our delightful feast.
Leader: You anoint my head with oil.
People: This is our consecration.
Leader: My cup overflows.

People: This is our abundance.

Leader: Surely goodness and mercy shall follow me all the days of my life.

People: And we shall dwell in the house of the Lord throughout eternity. This is our good news. (Trumpet B)

Musical Suggestions for The Fourth Sunday of Easter

Hymns for the Day

Title	AAHH	AME	AMEZ	LEVS	LMGM	YL	HG
All Hail the Power of Jesus' Name (CORONATION)	•	4	32	•	88	10	•
All Hail the Power of Jesus' Name (DIADEM)	293	5	33	•	89	•	•
All Hail the Power of Jesus' Name (MILES LANE)	294	6	34	•	•	•	•
Christ Is Made the Sure Foundation	•	518	•	•	•	•	•
He Leadeth Me, O Blessed Thought	142	395	292	•	•	391	•
O Thou In Whose Presence	422	83	454	•	•	•	•
The Lord Is My Shepherd	426	206	74	104	152	•	•

Spirituals	AAHH	AME	AMEZ	LEVS	LMGM	YL	HG
Let Us Break Bread Together	686	530	338	152	135	30	•
Fix Me, Jesus	436	•	•	125	314	•	•

Gospel Selections	AAHH	AME	AMEZ	LEVS	LMGM	YL	HG
God Is	134	•	•	•	•	•	•
The Lamb	179	•	•	•	•	•	•

Anthems

Psalm 23 *Eugene W. Hancock*

My Shepherd Will Supply My Need *Virgil Thomson*

My Eternal King *Jane Marshall*

The King of Love My Shepherd Is

Gospel Selections

The Good Shepherd *V. Michael McKay*

Organ Music

Benedictus *Max Reger*

Benedictus *Alec Rowley*

The Lord's My Shepherd, I'll Not Want *Barbara Harbach* (from *Augsburg Organ Library–Easter*)

The Fifth Sunday of Easter

Appropriate Banner and Altar Colors: White
Year A: Acts 7: 55-60/ Psalm 31: 1-16/ 1 Peter 2: 2-10/ John 14: 1-14
Year B: Acts 8: 26-40/ Psalm 22: 25-31/ 1 John 4: 7:-21/John 15: 1-8
Year C: Acts 11: 1-18/ Psalm 148/ Revelation 21: 1-6/ John 13: 31-35

Focus

The theme for these passages can be summed up in one simple word: mercy. God's compassion, benevolence, long-suffering, and genuine kindness towards generations of humans who continually and perpetually turn their backs, walk away, and have affairs with other gods is evidenced in the sending of The Only Begotten to die in our stead! Mercy is something that we cannot earn. Mercy is a quality we have no right to receive. Mercy is the essence of going past what is due us and providing something greater for us. Mercy is the very depth of God's amazing love for the created world.

The new Church in Acts sees this mercy in Stephen, who like Christ, allows himself to be stoned and prays for his murderers forgiveness as he breathes out his last breath. The Apostle Philip shows God's mercy as he is guided by The Holy Spirit to extend Christ to the Ethiopian official, an outsider. Gentiles who don't keep kosher laws are received by the Apostle Peter, and the Jewish Church sees the mercy of God extended outside of their circle. Mercy is evident through loving acceptance. Jesus was so filled with mercy until he gave up his divinity to share our common lot and offer us eternal life. He is the True Vine of God's deep love. He has shown us the way. We are the branches. And to go where he now exists in eternity, we must be as loving and as merciful to others. This is our call to bear fruit, which gives our merciful God much glory. Where is the fruit? This is the question that is not up for debate!

Visual aids

Flags of every nation might adorn your altar this Sunday as we celebrate God's mercy, which is now extended beyond the Jewish nation to "whosoever will come!" Grapes with vines attached, tree branches, and budding plants all address the theme of bearing the fruit of merciful love. The overhead might show various scenes of acts and deeds of mercy being performed by people who staff the different outreach ministries of your local congregation.

Call to Confession

We love because God first loved us. Those who say they love God and hate their brothers or sisters are liars. For we cannot love God whom we have not seen, and hate those we see each day. Let us confess our sin.

Confession

Almighty God, Lover of our souls, we come to you with ruptured relationships everywhere. Breathe upon us the breath of new life. Forgive us our sin. Help us to love in deeds that reveal your presence in our life. Empower us to walk in the new life of The Christ, in whose name we pray.

Words of Assurance

God abides in everyone who dares to confess that Jesus is The Son of God. With our confession, we now abide in God's love. This is good news.

Musical Suggestions for The Fifth Sunday of Easter

Hymns for the Day

Title	AAHH	AME	AMEZ	LEVS	LMGM	YL	HG
Christ for the World We Sing	•	565	•	•	•	•	•
Christ Is Made the Sure Foundation	•	518	•	•	•	•	•
Glorious Things of Thee Are Spoken	•	521	306	•	•	•	•
I Need Thee Every Hour	451	327	466	192	•	305	•
Make Me a Blessing	•	•	•	158	278	356	•
O Jesus I Have Promised	•	280	472	•	•	•	•

Spirituals	AAHH	AME	AMEZ	LEVS	LMGM	YL	HG
I Want to Be Ready	600	510	607	7	•	•	•
Soon and Very Soon	193	•	•	•	4	•	•
Woke Up This Morning	566	•	•	•	•	344	•
Oh, Lord Have Mercy	448	•	•	•	•	•	•

Gospel Selections	AAHH	AME	AMEZ	LEVS	LMGM	YL	HG
Your Grace and Mercy	270	•	•	•	•	•	•

Anthems

Now Glad of Heart *Sam Batt Owens*

I Am the Vine *Allen Pote*

The Vine Most Surely I Am *Heinrich Schütz*

Light's Glittering Morn Bedecks the Sky *Horatio W. Parker*

Spirituals

Any How *arr. Evelyn LaRue Simpson*
  (No. 11, *The Oxford Book of Spirituals*)

Organ Music

Aria *Charles Callahan*

Have Mercy Upon Me, O God, BWV 115 *Johann S. Bach*

O God of Mercy, God of Light *David Cherwien* (from *Interpretations, Book I*)

The Sixth Sunday of Easter

Appropriate Banner and Altar Colors: White
Year A: Acts 17: 22-31/ Psalm 66: 8-20/ 1 Peter 3: 13-22/John 14: 15-21
Year B: Acts 10: 44-48/ Psalm 98/ 1 John 5: 1-6/ John 15: 9-17
Year C: Acts 16: 9-15/ Psalm 67/ Revelation 21: 10, 22-22: 5/ John 14: 23-29

Focus

Obedience is the key to a right relationship with God, through Jesus Christ! The power of The Holy Spirit provides us with the will, the way, and the desire to obey God's command to love the whole world. Rebellion against God's law is what got the world into the shape it's in today. Our original parents decided to do things their own way and we became separated from God. Jesus is our at-one-ment (atonement)! The only way back to God is through the atoning work of Jesus at Calvary. Everyone is welcome to come through the blood and be restored to a loving relationship. It makes no difference how we feel about them, their bloodlines, their ethnicity, their tribal habits, or the color of their skin. God makes us all. God loves us all. God desires that all of us be saved and spend eternity as family in The Holy City, which Jesus has prepared.

Many are searching for God. There is a deep void within each one of us that needs to be "at home," with God residing on the throne of our heart. Paul found that seekers had built an altar to "the unknown God" as they sought inner fulfillment. Our job is to declare the name of Jesus and make God known throughout the world. Seekers are everywhere. As Paul went to the place of known prayer in Europe, he found a group of women, praying at the water. Lydia, a wealthy entrepreneur, and her group of women friends heed Paul's message. She extended herself to the apostle, embraced the good news of Jesus Christ, and became the founder of one of the first house churches in "the new world." Paul obeyed the Holy Spirit's lead, despite the resistance of the other Jewish disciples. The Holy Spirit always pushes our growing edges.

Visual Aids

Doves, signs of The Holy Spirit amidst signs of flames and a flowing water fall, indicate the way that God sends us, empowered by The Holy Spirit to speak new words that bring new believers to baptism. Plants with long vines also address the way that the Living Word spreads.

Call to Confession

The love of God calls us to obey every commandment. Since we have broken the commandments, it is our time to confess.

Confession

God, the Ancestors used to say that all you told them to do, they did not do. Then, they said that all you told them not to do, they did. We laughed as they confessed. We have now become them. Forgive us our sin. Help us to show you our love through the gift of The Christ we pray.

Words of Assurance

Everyone who believes that Jesus is the Christ has been born of God, and everyone who loves the parent loves the child. By this we know that when we love God and obey God's commandments, then we love the Children of God. This is our time of new beginning.

Musical Suggestions for The Sixth Sunday of Easter

Hymns for the Day

Title	AAHH	AME	AMEZ	LEVS	LMGM	YL	HG
At Calvary	246	•	•	•	•	275	•
Come, Holy Ghost	•	•	•	112	69	•	•
Come, Thou Fount of Every Blessing	175	77	29	111	•	9	•
Shall We Gather At the River	•	486	562	141	103	•	•
Trust and Obey	380	377	443	205	•	334	•
Victory in Jesus	261	•	638	•	240	98	•

Anthems

An Easter Anthem *Christopher Boodle*

If Ye Love Me, Keep My Commandments
  Thomas Tallis

O Speak to Me of Jesus' Sorrow *Johann G. Gebhard*

Spirituals

You Better Mind *Jester Hairston*

I'll Never Turn Back No More *R. Nathaniel Dett*

I'll Never Turn Back No Mo' *Hall Johnson*

Gospel Selections

Integrity *V. Michael McKay*

Refreshed in His Presence *V. Michael McKay*

Take Away *V. Michael McKay*

Organ Music

Variations on NETTLETON *Undine Smith Moore* (Anthology of African American Organ Music, Volume 2)

5 Easter Season Hymn Improvisations *Michael Burkhardt*

Ascension Sunday

Appropriate Banner and Altar Colors: White

Year A, B, and C: Acts 1: 1-11, Psalm 47/ Ephesians 1: 15-23/ Luke 24: 44-53

Focus

We return to another time of waiting! Yet we are blessed to wait in this season with blessed hope. For fifty days after the resurrection, Jesus has been making various appearances to show the disciples that indeed he had risen from the dead. Finally they had been convinced, and began to feel that the Messiah was about to bring in the revolution for which all Jews had looked for over the centuries. They were tired of being last, least, and "little" in the political arenas. They wanted to be first. They wanted positions of power. They wanted to be in charge. Now was most certainly the time. Jesus had defeated death. Jesus had overcome the grave. Jesus had risen in spite of the crucifixion. The crowd that has assembled at Bethany now waits for their new political agenda. And Jesus "ordered them not to leave Jerusalem, but to wait for the promise" of The Holy Spirit. (Acts 1: 4)

The Holy Spirit, the comforter, the power, the one who will live inside and walk alone side of every believer, is coming if we wait. The Holy Spirit, who will remind us of the ministry mission of Jesus and provide us with direction to carry it on, will give us wisdom, understanding, and knowledge if we wait. The Holy Spirit will be sent to the disciples to be the courage, the Boldness, and the love that they will need to do the new work assigned their hands if they will simply go to Jerusalem and wait. Then Jesus, the Christ, lifted his hands and gave them a benediction of blessing and was elevated into heaven on a cloud saying, "Mission accomplished!"

Visual Aids

Globes and maps will convey the message that Jesus is Lord over the whole wide world. Various types of shells lying sprinkled around the altar represent the various types of baptisms that bring forth new Christians into the global Church of God. An overhead picture of many different types of church buildings across the world will address the message that The Holy Spirit is empowering all who believe.

Responsive Reading

Leader: It's hand-clapping time for the Getting Up God!

People: There will be no willy, nilly, pitty pat clapping either!

Leader: Give it up, for the God who got up!

People: Make some noise for the One who destroyed sin, death, and hell.

Leader: Call out a shout for The Awesome God, who breaks through earth and lifts above clouds.

People: Jesus lifted off in visible sight.

Leader: That gave a new song to those who had been singing the blues!

People: Jesus overcame stormy weather and rose above every cloud.

Leader: Blessed assurance, Jesus is exalted over the earth.

People: Singing breaks out among the people of this getting up God!

(Trumpet B)

Musical Suggestions for Ascension Sunday

Hymns for the Day

Title	AAHH	AME	AMEZ	LEVS	LMGM	YL	HG
Alleluia! Sing to Jesus	•	•	•	•	67	•	•
Look, Ye Saints, the Sight Is Glorious	•	181	•	•	•	•	•
I Am on the Battlefield	480	390	•	•	281	•	•

Gospel Selections	AAHH	AME	AMEZ	LEVS	LMGM	YL	HG
Go!	•	•	•	•	66	•	•

Anthems

God Is Gone Up *Arthur Hutchings*

Celebration Alleluia *Marvin Curtis*

Let All the World *Ralph Vaughan Williams* (From *Five Mystical Songs*)

The Lord Ascendeth Up on High *Leo Sowerby*

Achieved is the Glorious Work *F. J. Haydn*

Spirituals

My Good Lord's Done Been Here arr. *Lee Cloud* (No. 2, *Oxford Book of Spirituals*)

In Bright Mansions Above arr. *Roland Carter*

Organ Music

Gwine Up to View duh Heav'nly Land *William Farley Smith* (from *Songs of Deliverance*)

Le Ascension *Oliver Messiaen*

The Seventh Sunday of Easter

Appropriate Banner and Altar Colors: White
Year A: Acts 1: 6-14/ Psalm 68: 1-10, 32-35/ 1 Peter 4: 12-14; 5: 6-11/ John 17: 1-11
Year B: Acts 1: 15-17, 21-26/ Psalm 1/ 1 John 5: 9-13/ John 17: 6-19
Year C: Acts 16: 16-34/ Psalm 94/Revelation 22: 12-21/John 17: 20-26

Focus

"Somebody prayed for me. Had me on their mind. Took the time to pray for me. I'm so glad they prayed." The songwriter addresses the great act of every believer, that of praying for others. Jesus gives us the model; for it was a fervent deed that he practiced. He often slipped away and spent time in prayer. Prayer is not an option for us. Prayer is not simply for when we and "ours" are in need. Prayer is not some ritual to be preserved for the lofty and the pious. Prayer is a gift that allows us access into the throne room and gives us an audience with The Almighty.

Jesus, on his way to the Cross, takes time to pray for The Church. Jesus, knowing that his death was certain, takes the time to commend us to the keeping power of God. Jesus, realizing that this earthly mission was near completion, knelt down and asked God to bless us, to keep us, to empower us, so that his mission ministry might not be in vain. It is our job to keep this prayer chain alive. It is our duty to unite our hearts in prayer for those already in the Church as well as for those who need to come. We are to keep an attitude of prayer. We are to stay on alert for needs around us that require prayer. We are to whisper prayers all day long. For it is in Christ that we live, move, and have our being. So, prayer is an extension of our loving relationship with the One who has already prayed for us and now sits on the right hand of God, being our cheerleader as the Holy Spirit makes our intercession. For pray as we must and might, we don't know how to pray! Thank God for the Holy Spirit, who takes our request and makes them intelligent unto God! And God is only a prayer away!

Visual aids

Different models of praying hands on the altar make a powerful statement on this day. The overhead might show different photos of people praying both together and alone. Make sure to include pictures of both children, teens, and young adults gathered in prayer. They need our encouragement to continue the habit of prayer throughout their school careers.

Benediction

Leader: God sends you into the world. Go! Keep alert for the adversary of our souls is looking for someone to devour.
People: We go, steadfast in our faith, for we know God. And we know that our brothers and sisters in the world are undergoing the same kinds of suffering and tests. We will hold them in our prayers.
Leader: God sends you into the world. Go, because the spirit of glory, which is the Spirit of God, is resting upon us! The Holy Spirit intercedes for us.
People: We go, in the power of the Word and the Name.
Leader: The Strong Name of God, the Salvation of Jesus Christ and the Power of the Holy Spirit goes before us. Amen.

(Trumpet A)

Musical Suggestions for The Seventh Sunday of Easter

Hymns for the Day

Title	AAHH	AME	AMEZ	LEVS	LMGM	YL	HG
In Me	452	•	•	•	•	•	•
Just a Little Talk with Jesus	378	351	•	83	211	•	•
Sweet Hour of Prayer	442	307	446	178	212	304	•
The Beautiful Garden of Prayer	425	319	•	•	•	308	•
Thy Way, O Lord	444	311	•	•	39	•	•
What a Friend (CONVERSE)	431	323	282	109	214	342	•

Spirituals	AAHH	AME	AMEZ	LEVS	LMGM	YL	HG
Come Here, Jesus, If You Please	439	•	•	163	•	•	•
King Jesus Is a-Listen'	364	•	•	84	•	•	•
Standin' in the Need of Prayer	441	•	416	177	216	310	•
Steal Away	546	489	611	103	319	•	•

Gospel Selections	AAHH	AME	AMEZ	LEVS	LMGM	YL	HG
A Praying Spirit	458	•	•	•	213	340	•
Even Me	457	•	463	167	138	416	•
Somebody Prayed for Me	505	•	•	•	•	•	•
What a Friend (ANNIE LOWERY)	430	•	•	•	•	•	•

Anthems

Our Father *John W. Work*
The Lord's Prayer *Albert Malotte*
Our Father Who Art in Heaven, BWV 760/761 *Johann S. Bach*
The Lord's Prayer *Cecil B. Gates*
Almighty God, of Our Fathers *Will James*
Prière *Henri Mulet*

Spirituals

Jesus, Lay Your Head in the Window *Joseph Joubert*
King Jesus is A-Listening *William L. Dawson*

Organ Music

Steal Away to Jesus *arr. David Hurd*
Steal Away to Jesus *arr. Raymond Haan*
Sonata No. 6 *Felix Mendelssohn*
Variations on "Kum Ba Yah" *Michael Behenke*

PENTECOST

Pentecost

The Holy Spirit arrives fresh, hot, touching, laughing, anointing, and dispatching the hidden and scared individuals into the streets. The Holy Spirit, the comforter, sent to live in us, work on us, walk beside us to guide our daily life, comes on the scene. It's time for celebration. It's a distinct and significant occasion, for power is in the house! It's a brand new day, a brand new beginning, and a brand new season of growth, spread, and change.

"You'll receive power" is the promise of Acts 1: 8. The Holy Spirit's power is necessary for the effective living of our new life in Christ. The acts and deeds of those called Christian will be noticed by all the world. The power to make a difference is ours!

Altar Focus

For Pentecost, red with white paraments (altar and pulpit coverings) and red balloons are needed to set the stage for fire, which not only burns and consumes, but ignites, motivates, and inspires. Red candles of assorted sizes and shapes would make a lovely addition. A banner with tongues of fire laid across the altar can assist in delivering the message of a brand new day.

Pentecost Sunday

Appropriate Banner and Altar Colors: Red

Year A: Acts 2: 1-21/ (or, Numbers 11: 24-30) Psalm 104: 24-35/ 1 Corinthians 12: 3-13/ John 20: 19-23

Year B: Acts 2: 1-21 (or, Ezekiel 37: 1-14) / Psalm 104: 24-35/ Romans 8: 22-27/ John 15: 26-27; 16: 4-15

Year C: Acts 2: 1-21/ (or, Genesis 11: 1-9) Psalm 104: 24-35/ Romans 8: 14-17/John 14: 8-27

Focus

The "live in God" moves into the spirits of the disciples! They are touched, kissed, made bold, and empowered to leave the place of waiting and hiding to go and take the message of the Risen Savior into all the world. The wait is over! The power has arrived. The paraclete, or the helper of the helpless, and the agent on assignment from God has come. Things will be different. Things cannot remain the same. Transformation is in the house! A revolution has broken out and cannot be contained. Possibilities never imagined come to mind. Opportunities for witness never conceived appear. People are in the city from all the known world, and they come to hear the wild faith-filled witness of those who have been sent down into the world with a message of loving acceptance. They look foolish. People think they are drunk. They sound crazy. Yet many others believe their message. They become soul winners. The Church of the Living God grows that day...it has continued...it will continue! Thanks be unto God for this uncontrollable fire!

Call to Worship

Leader: People of God, I proclaim that this is the day of God's latter rain!

People: Rain, fall upon these dry and arid bones.

Leader: People of God, I decree that the still dew of refreshing will penetrate our thirsty souls.

People: Dew, descend upon our parched places.

Leader: People of God, I declare that God will breathe upon us that we might fully live.

People: Breathe upon us and fill us with new and abundant life. We gather, ready to receive!

Leader: This is the day of Pentecost, the rain, the dew, and the fresh wind of God is present to minister to every need.

People: Spirit Holy, fall fresh upon us!

CALL TO CONFESSION

Our lives are evidence of the dryness that overtakes and stifles creativity. Dry lives are prone to sin. God has given us the right and the ability to prophesy to the four winds that they may come and impart new life in order that we might live pleasing to God. This is our time of confession. Let us pray.

CONFESSION

God, our bones are dried up and our hope is lost; we are cut off from you. We repent of our sin. We seek your forgiveness and grace. Rain upon us. Breathe upon us. Save us from ourselves, we pray in the name of The Living Christ.

WORDS OF ASSURANCE

The promise from God is alive and well. "O my people, I will put my spirit within you and you shall live, and I will place you on your own soil that you might know that I, the Lord, have spoken and I will act." This is certainly good news.

RESPONSIVE READING

Leader: Keeping it together is a difficult thing for most folks!

People: Now, that's on the real side! For we struggle to piece together our lives!

Leader: Yet on the day of Pentecost, a group of scared folks got it together.

People: And the Holy Spirit was dispatched from heaven with signs and wonders.

Leader: Suddenly there was the sound of wind and the sighting of divided tongues of fire.

People: The people were bewildered, amazed, and astonished as they were filled with fresh power.

Leader: May the glory of the Lord endure forever!

People: We have received mightily from The Lord.

Leader: With the coming of the Holy Spirit we are renewed.

People: With the coming of the Holy Spirit, we are sent forth into the world.

Leader: May the Lord rejoice in the way we live our spirit- filled lives.

People: May our meditation always be pleasing unto God. We will bless the Lord. And we will work diligently to keep it together. The power is ours. Thanks be unto God!

OFFERTORY INVITATION

The coming of the Holy Spirit indicated that the new Church had to grow up and take full responsibility for the Realm of God. That mandate has reached us. Let us give generously so that The Holy Spirit may reach many others.

OFFERTORY PRAISE

The Advocate has come, and God, we give you praise. The Holy Spirit testifies in our hearts of your amazing grace toward us. So we give in order to simply say thanks! Receive our gifts in the name of Christ, we pray.

BENEDICTION

Leader: Christ told his followers that it was to their advantage that he go away so that the Comforter might come.

People: The Spirit of Comfort goes before us into the world.

Leader: Christ told his followers that there were many things they did not fully understand.

People: The Spirit of Truth has come to speak to our hearts and to lead us in right paths.

Leader: Go into the world, enfolded in the Triune God, Creator, Redeemer, and Sustainer.

People: Hallelujah and Amen. (Trumpet, B)

MUSICAL SUGGESTIONS FOR PENTECOST

HYMNS FOR THE DAY

Title	AAHH	AME	AMEZ	LEVS	LMGM	YL	HG
For Your Gift of God the Spirit	•	•	•	•	•	•	45
Spirit of God Descend upon My Heart	312	189	224	119	74	187	•
Come, Holy Spirit, Heavenly Dove	314	191	210	•	•	191	•
Sweet, Sweet Spirit	326	196	218	120	75	192	•
The Comforter Has Come	•	199	•	•	•	190	•
Something within	493	353	630	•	•	454	•
Holy Spirit, Flow Through Me	•	•	•	•	73	198	•
Send the Fire	•	•	•	•	•	415	•
Waiting on the Lord	•	•	•	•	•	414	•
Go Forth for God	•	•	392	•	•	•	•

Spirituals	AAHH	AME	AMEZ	LEVS	LMGM	YL	HG
Everytime I Feel the Spirit	325	•	220	114	220	311	•

Gospel Selections	AAHH	AME	AMEZ	LEVS	LMGM	YL	HG
Just Like Fire	•	•	•	•	•	511	•
Anointing	318	•	•	•	•	•	•
Let It Breathe on Me	316	295	225	116	71	412	•
Holy Spirit	319	•	•	•	•	•	•
Go!	•	•	•	•	66	•	•

Anthems

Spirit of the Living God *Daniel Iverson/*
    arr. Malcolm Kogut
I Will Sing with the Spirit *John Rutter*

Breathe on Me, Breath of God
Lord, Send Out Your Spirit *Alexander Peloquin*
Come, Holy Ghost, Draw Near Us *Leo Sowerby*

Spirituals

Everytime I Feel the Spirit *William Dawson*
Holy Spirit, Don't You Leave Me *William Grant Still*
Witness *arr. Jack Halloran*
    (No. 20, *Oxford Book of Spirituals*)

Everytime I Feel the Spirit *Moses Hogan*
I'm Gonna Sing 'Til the Spirit Moves in My Heart
    Moses Hogan

Gospel Selections

Sanctify Me *V. Michael McKay*
Since He Came Into My Life *Lena McLin*

Refreshed in His Presence *V. Michael McKay*

Organ Music

Who'll be a Witness fo' Mah Lawd? *William Farley Smith* (from Songs of Deliverance)
Veni Creator Spiritus *Everett Titcomb*
Like a Murmur of the Dove's Song *James Biery* (from *Augsburg Organ Library–Easter*)
Toccata *John Weaver*
Prelude on "Come, Holy Spirit, Our Souls Inspire" *Leo Sowerby*
Prelude, Adagio et Choral Varié on "Veni Creator" *Maurice Durufle*
Komm Gott Schòpfer, BWV 631, 667, 651, 652 *Johann S. Bach*

A Music Worship Worksheet

Date: _____

Season of the Church Year: _____

Hebrew Scripture: _____

Psalm: _____

Epistle: _____

Gospel Leader: _____

1. What are the major images that rise from these readings? _____
_____
_____
_____

2. What is the major challenge in your life presently? _____
_____
_____
_____

3. Personal Leader: _____
_____
_____
_____

4. Choir related: _____
_____
_____
_____
_____

Permission granted from GIA Publications, Inc. to photocopy the worksheet as necessary.

5. Congregational Leader: _____

6. Social environment: _____

7. What hope is offered to you from God's Word for Sunday? _____

8. What music speaks to these scriptures for you? _____

9. What does the Living Word invite the People of God to do? _____

10. What anthems relay these passages? _____

11. What are the major issues facing the people in scriptures? _____

Permission granted from GIA Publications, Inc. to photocopy the worksheet as necessary.

12. How are the issues relevant to your local congregation? _____
_____
_____
_____

13. What music speaks to these contemporary issues? _____
_____
_____
_____

14. What is surprising/unexpected to you in these passages? _____
_____
_____
_____

15. What is comforting to you? _____
_____
_____
_____

16. What is the music that will be a call to worship for this service? _____
_____
_____
_____

17. What gospel song touches these passages? _____
_____
_____
_____

18. What contemporary music addresses these scriptures? _____
_____
_____
_____

Permission granted from GIA Publications, Inc. to photocopy the worksheet as necessary.

19. Is there a piece of music that the Praise Dance Team might consider? _____
_____
_____
_____

20. How does the altar, banners, and overhead assist the congregation with "getting" the message? _____
_____
_____
_____

21. How can you tie these scriptures in with the title of the pastor's message? _____
_____
_____
_____

Additional comments: _____
_____
_____
_____
_____
_____
_____
_____
_____
_____
_____
_____
_____
_____
_____
_____
_____

Permission granted from GIA Publications, Inc. to photocopy the worksheet as necessary.

Appendix of Resources

1. The Mass of Saint Augustine

A Gospel Mass for Congregation, SATB Choir, and Piano by Leon C. Roberts

Publisher:

GIA Publications, Inc.

7404 South Mason Avenue, Chicago, IL 60638

Telephone: 1 800 442 1358 • FAX: 708 496 3828 • www.giamusic.com or custserv@giamusic.com

Publisher Catalog Numbers:

G-2448	Complete SATB Choral/Vocal Score	564-F	Congregation Card
MS-160	Stereo Recording		

The Mass of St. Augustine/individual Octavo Editions:

G-2468	Thank you, Lord (Opening Song)	G-2507	Lord, Have Mercy (Kyrie)
G-2469	Glory to God (Gloria)	G-2470	Let Us Go Rejoicing
G-2471	Alleluia	G-2472	Eucharistic Prayer Acclamations (Sanctus, Memorial Acclamation and Doxology)
G-2473	The Lord's Prayer		
G-2474	Lamb of God (Agnus Dei)		
G-2475	Remember Me		
G-2476	He Has the Power		

General Comments:

- Excellent, accessible way to introduce Mass setting
- Movements are relatively easy and short
- Frequent use of easy homophonic, "hymn-like" writing
- Effective relationship between dynamics and text
- Could be used with bass guitar and drum set on any or all movements
- Tenor reads in same treble clef (shared) as sopranos and altos at times
- Entire Mass offered as separate octavos from publisher

2. The Mass of Saint Martin de Porres

A Gospel Mass for Congregation, SATB Choir, Soli, and Piano by Leon C. Roberts

*(Orchestra Scores available from Publisher)

Publisher:

Oregon Catholic Press Publications

5536 Northeast Hassalo Street, Portland, Oregon 97213

1-800-LITURGY or 1-877-596-1653 • www.ocp.org or 1iturgy@ocp.org

Publisher Catalog Numbers:

10393	Complete SATB Choral/Vocal Score

Professional Recordings Available from:

GIA Publications, Inc.

7404 South Mason Avenue, Chicago, IL 60638

Telephone: 1 800 442 1358 • FAX: 708 496 3828 • www.giamusic.com or custserv@giamusic.com

CD-342 Compact Disc Recording • CS-342 Cassette Recording

The Mass of St. Martin de Porres:

I Call Upon You, God! (Gathering Song)	Lord, Have Mercy (Kyrie)
Glory to God in the Highest (Gloria)	Taste and See the Goodness of the Lord
Alleluia (Gospel Acclamation)	(Responsorial Psalm)
General Intercessions	I Surrender All
Holy, Holy, Holy (Sanctus)	Keep In Mind (Memorial Acclamation)
Great Amen	The Lord's Prayer/Doxology
Lamb of God (Agnus Dei)	Jesus Is Here Right Now (Communion Hymn)
Mary's Canticle	His Eye Is On the Sparrow (Meditation Hymn),
Give Us Peace (Sending Forth)	arr. Jeffrey LaValley

Individual Octavo Editions Available from Oregon Catholic Press:

10397	Give Us Peace (Sending Forth)	10398	I Surrender All
10399	Jesus Is Here Right Now	10400	Taste and See the Goodness of the Lord
10449	His Eye is On the Sparrow, arr. Jeffrey LaValley		

Individual Octavo Editions Available from GIA Publications, Inc.

G-4327	I Call Upon You, God!	G-3826	Mary's Canticle

General Comments:
- Involves styles ranging from Gregorian chant to contemporary gospel
- Congregation parts are easy as to encourage participation
- Reflects on the universality of both Catholic and Protestant traditions
- Syncopated and filled with rhythmic energy
- Somewhat lengthy movements
- Almost 1/2 of this mass is available as separate octavos

3. The Mass of Saint Cyprian

A Gospel Mass for Congregation, SATB Choir, Soli, and Piano by Kenneth W. Louis
*(Orchestra Scores available from Publisher)

Publisher:

GIA Publications, Inc.

7404 South Mason Avenue, Chicago, IL 60638

Telephone: 1 800 442 1358 • FAX: 708 496 3828 • www.giamusic.com or custserv@giamusic.com

Publisher Catalog Numbers:

G-5173	Complete SATB Choral/Vocal Score	613-F	Assembly (Congregation) Edition
CD-462	Compact Disc Recording	CS-462	Cassette Recording

The Mass of St. Cyprian:

- The Procession: The Lord Will Hear the Just
- Glory To God (Gloria)
- Gospel Acclamation: Alleluia
- Preface Acclamation: Holy, Holy (Sanctus)
- Great Amen
- Our Father (The Lord's Prayer)
- Communion Hymn: Taste and See
- Lord Have Mercy (Kyrie)
- Responsorial Psalm: Proclaim God's Marvelous Deeds
- Offertory: I'm Willing Lord
- Memorial Acclamation: Dying you Destroyed Our Death
- Lamb of God (Agnus Dei)
- Jesus, You Brought Me All the Way

Individual Octavo Editions:

G-5637	Communion Hymn: Taste and See	G-5142	The Procession and Responsorial Psalm (The Lord Will Hear the Just/Proclaim God's Marvelous Deeds)

General Comments:

- Call and Response used throughout
- Rich, stately choral writing
- Almost entirely homophonic; some unison singing; not to rhythmically involved
- Movements are short; appropriate for worship service in separate parts or in small groups
- Varied styles, tempi, and key signatures
- Piano part accessible and lends itself to additional improvisation as musician or conductor sees fit

4. Alpha Mass, Opus 30

A Gospel Mass for SATB Choir, Soli, and Piano by Glenn Burleigh
*(Orchestra Scores available from Publisher)

Publisher:

Glenn Burleigh Music Workshop and Ministry, Inc.
Post Office Box 16901, Oklahoma City, OK 73113
405 842 3470—Music Orders • 405 232 7477—Administrative Offices • wwwglenmusik.com or glenmusik@aol.com

Publisher Catalog Numbers:

- Complete Choral/Vocal Score
- Full Orchestral Score (Conductor's Edition)
- Cassette Recording
- Instrumental/Orchestral Parts

Alpha Mass:

- The Gathering
- Kyrie (Lord, Have Mercy)
- Matthew, Mark, Luke, And John
- Credo (I Believe)
- Create In Me A Clean Heart
- Gloria (Gloria)
- Alleluia
- Sanctus (Holy)

Memorial Acclamation
For The Kingdom (The "Our Father")
Joy
Go In Peace

Do This In Remembrance Of Me
Agnus Dei (Lamb of God)
There's A King On the Throne

Individual Octavo Editions Available from Publisher:

Do This In Remembrance Of Me Gloria

General Comments:
- English and Latin texts; Divided into four (4) section
- Classical, jazz, and gospel styles represented
- Medium-Difficult
- Movements tied together with textual theme of "Unity in the Kingdom" of God
- Able to actively include congregation in several areas
- Excellent performance suggestions and descriptions of each section provided by composer

5. Gospel Mass

A Mass Setting for SATB Choir, Soli, and Piano by Robert Ray
*(Orchestra Scores available from Composer)

Publisher:

Jenson Publications/Hal Leonard Publications
7777 West Bluemound Road, Post Office Box 13819, Milwaukee, WI 53213 • 414 774 3630 • www.halleonard.com
*Does not accept orders online

Publisher Catalog Numbers:

HL44707014	Complete SAT13 Choral/Vocal Score	HL08740901	CID Recording

Gospel Mass:

KYRIE—Lord Have Mercy
CREDO—I Believe in God
SANCTUS—Holy, Holy Lord of Hosts

GLORIA—Glory to God in the Highest
ACCLAMATION—Hallelujah Praise the Lord
AGNUS DEI—Lamb of God

Individual Octavo Editions:

HL08595487   CREDO—I Believe in God   HL08595483   ACCLAMATION—Hallelujah Praise the Lord

Instrumental Accompaniment Recordings:

HL08740900   Gospel Mass [SHOWTRAX CASSETTE]   HL08740901   Gospel Mass [SHOWTRAX CD]

General Comments:
- One of the most popular gospel settings of the Ordinary
- Nice integration of solo material within the choral writing
- Mostly homophonic, with use of divisi
- Nice for Easter/Lent or Christmas/Advent

...ntion to dynamic contrast in repeated sections
...ed for orchestra
... and Percussion parts included in SATB vocal score
...sation encouraged for soloists and musicians

6. Lamentation and Celebration, Opus 43

A Commissioned Work in Memory of the Oklahoma City Bombing of April 19, 1995, by Glenn Burleigh
for SATB Choir, Brass Choir, Bass, Percussion/Timpani, Piano and Organ
*(Orchestra Scores available from Publisher)

Publisher:
Glenn Burleigh Music Workshop and Ministry, Inc.
Post Office Box 16901, Oklahoma City, OK 73113
405 842 3470—Music Orders • 405 232 7477—Administrative Offices • wwwglenmusik.com or glenmusik@aol.com

Publisher Catalog Numbers:

Complete Choral/Vocal Score	[Item #GB1001-A] Cassette Recording
Full Score (Conductor's Edition)	Instrumental/Orchestral Parts
Orchestral Arrangement (coming soon!)	

Lamentation and Celebration:

Mercy	Happiness
Trouble	Deliverance
Joy	

Individual Octavo Editions Available from Publisher: None

General Comments:
- Medium-Difficult, divisi writing
- Elements of gospel/jazz throughout; makes use of medieval chant-like passages; imitative fugue-like areas
- Uses tympani, organ pedals, and lower register of piano to dramatize tragedy; bomb blast is written in score as well as flashing red lights, sirens, and "screams in the crowd."
- Movements could be performed separately, but would work better together for dramatic impact
- Happiness—Excellent anthem for Sunday morning worship service
- Emotions of the piece re-enforced through rhythm and dynamics

7. The Coming

A Celebration of Advent and Christmas for SATB Choir, Soli, Congregation, Piano, Organ, Percussion, Lead/Bass Guitar by Leon C. Roberts
*(Orchestra Scores available from Publisher)

Publisher:
Oregon Catholic Press Publications
5536 Northeast Hassalo Street, Portland, Oregon 97213
1-800-LITURGY or 1-877-596-1653 • www.ocp.org or liturgy@ocp.org

Publisher Catalog Numbers:

#10403	Complete Choral/Vocal Score	#10404	Cassette Recording
	*with instrumental parts	#10405	Compact Disc Recording
Full Orchestral Score (Conductor's Edition)			
Instrumental/Orchestral Parts			

The Coming:

Come, Lord Jesus, Come!	Kyrie
Lord, Make Us Turn To You	Alleluia
Wait On The Lord	Holy, Holy, Holy *Audio Sample Available
Memorial Acclamation	At Publisher's Website
Great Amen	Lord's Prayer and Doxology
Lamb of God	We Remember You
He Shall Be Called Wonderful	

Individual Octavo Editions Available From Publisher:

#10591	He Shall Be Called Wonderful
	*Audio Sample Available At Publisher's Website
#10783	Lord Make Us Turn To You
#11045	We Remember You

General Comments:
- Use of modal chant style; accessible homophonic singing, flavored with gospel-styled rhythms; includes a "rap."
- Mass setting that calls for contemporary society to allow God to be born within each person
- Composer provides concise instructions for interpretation/style for even the novice musician
- Would be fitting for anytime of year

8. Born to Die, Opus 25

A Christmas Cantata for SATB Choir, Soli, and Piano by Glenn Burleigh

*(Orchestra Scores available from Publisher)

Publisher:

Glenn Burleigh Music Workshop and Ministry, Inc.

Post Office Box 16901, Oklahoma City, OK 73113

405 842 3470—Music Orders • 405 232 7477—Administrative Offices • wwwglenmusik.com or glenmusik@aol.com

Publisher Catalog Numbers:

- Complete Choral/Vocal Score
- Full Orchestral Score (Conductor's Edition)
- Cassette Tape Recording (2 tape set)
- Instrumental/Orchestral Parts

Born To Die:

- Born To Die
- The Travail
- Fear Not For Behold
- Go Back Another Way
- Mothers' Lament
- The Magnificat
- What's In A Name?
- With His Stripes We Are Healed
- Born To Die (Reprise)
- His Yoke Is Easy
- My Soul Doth Magnify The Lord (Song of Mary)
- Well, The Savior Is Born
- What Shall I Render? (Song of the Wise Men)
- Why Do The Heathen Rage? (Song of Herod)
- Not 'Til I've Seen Jesus (Song of Simeon)
- You Shall Be Free Indeed
- I Know That My Redeemer Liveth
- Keep-A Preachin' The Word
- The Song Of The Lord
- Hosanna

Individual Octavo Editions Available from Publisher:

- Born To Die
- My Soul Doth Magnify The Lord
- Hosanna
- The Magnificat
- His Yoke Is Easy
- Why Do the Heathen Rage? (Song of Herod)
- Keep-A Preachin' The Word
- What's In a Name

General Comments:

- Multiplicity of musical taste/styles
- Divided into two (2) sections, with scriptural references (narration)
- Rich choral passages that explore the vocal range
- Some challenging, imitative areas; frequent use of divisi
- Piano part is very technically involved; However, composer encourages improvisation throughout "freedom within structure"
- Excellent performance suggestions given by composer
- Could be performed as an oratorio or full-scale cantata (with drama, dance, and staging)

9. The Nguzo Saba Suite, Opus 41

A Kwanzaa Celebration for SATB Choir, Soli, and Piano by Glenn Burleigh

*(Orchestra Scores available from Publisher)

Publisher:

Glenn Burleigh Music Workshop and Ministry, Inc.

Post Office Box 16901, Oklahoma City, OK 73113

405 842 3470—Music Orders • 405 232 7477—Administrative Offices • wwwglenmusik.com or glenmusik@aol.com

Publisher Catalog Numbers:

Complete Choral/Vocal Score	[item #GB1001-A] Cassette Recording
Full Orchestral Score (Conductor's Edition)	Instrumental/Orchestral Parts

The Nguzo Saba Suite, Opus 41:

Umoja (Unity)	Kujichagulia (Self-Determination)
Ujima (Collective Work and Responsibility)	Ujamma (Cooperative Economics)
Nia (Purpose)	Kuumba (Creativity)
Imani (Faith) Finale	

Individual Octavo Editions Available From Publisher:

Nia	Ujima

General Comments:

- 30-35 minutes for entire work
- Medium-Difficult
- Movements 2-6 are strongly recommended by composer for church
- choir/worship
- Movements 1 and 7 are concert-like in nature and somewhat involved
- Chant-like in some areas; lyrical unison sections; interesting treatment of intervals (with descending fourths and parallel chordal movement)
- Dramatic use of dynamics
- Nia and Ujamma highly recommended for youth choirs

10. Let God Arise

An Easter Cantata for SATB Choir, Soli, and Piano by Glenn Burleigh

*(Orchestra Scores available from Publisher)

Publisher:

Glenn Burleigh Music Workshop and Ministry, Inc.

Post Office Box 16901, Oklahoma City, OK 73113

405 842 3470—Music Orders • 405 232 7477—Administrative Offices • wwwglenmusik.com or glenmusik@aol.com

Publisher Catalog Numbers:

Complete Choral/Vocal Score
Full Orchestral Score (Conductor's Edition)
Excerpts/9 Songs (Cassette)

Compact Disc Recording (2 CD Set)
Instrumental/Orchestral Parts

Let God Arise

Anoint Us
Prepare Me A Body (TTBB)
Hosanna, Hosanna
Do This In Remembrance Of Me
When Thou Comest
I'm Gonna 'Rise
You Must Be Born Again
Jesus Is
I'm Gonna Rise (Reprise)
When Jesus 'Rose
Let the Redeemed Say So

O For A Thousand Tongues To Sing
Follow Me
Song Of the Disciples
Give Us Barabbas/I Find No Fault
See How They Done My Lord
Faithful Over A Few Things
You Must Be Like A Child
What Does All This Mean?
Hallelujah, Hosanna (Reprise)
My Good Lord Done Been Here
Let God Arise

Sources: Books

Abbington, James. *Let Mt. Zion Rejoice! Music in the African American Church.* Valley Forge, PA: Judson Press, 2001.

Abbington, James., ed. *Readings in African American Church Music and Worship.* Chicago: GIA Publications, 2001.

Costen, Melva Wilson. *African American Christian Worship.* Nashville: Abingdon Press, 1993.

Dudley, Grenae D. and Carlyle F. Stewart III. *Sanfoka: Celebrations for the African-American Church.* Cleveland: United Church Press, 1997.

Garcia, William Burres. "Church Music by Black Composers: A Bibliography of Choral Music" in *Readings in African American Church Music and Worship.* Chicago: GIA Publications, 2001. pp 385–407.

Hollies, Linda H. *Trumpet in Zion: Worship Resources, Year A.* Cleveland: Pilgrim Press, 2001.

Kirk-Duggan, Cheryl A. *African American Special Days: 15 Complete Worship Services.* Nashville: Abingdon Press, 1996.

Mapson, Wendell J., Jr. *The Ministry of Music in the Black Church.* Valley Forge, PA: Judson Press, 1984.

McClain. William B. *Come Sunday: The Liturgy of Zion.* Nashville: Abingdon Press, 1990.

Talbot, Frederick H. *African American Worship: New Eyes for Seeing.* Lima, OH: Fairway Press, 1998.

Warren, Gwendolin Sims. *Ev'ry Time I Feel the Spirit: 101 Best-Loved Psalms, Gospel Hymns, and Spiritual Songs of the African-American Church.* New York: Henry Holt and Company, 1997.

White, Evelyn Davidson. *Choral Music by African American Composers: A Selected, Annotated Bibliography,* 2nd Edition. Lanham, MD: Scarecrow Press, 1996.

Sources: Websites

www.Choralnet.org	ChoralNet, USA
www.giamusic.com	GIA Publications, Inc., Chicago, IL
www.glennmusik.com	Glenn Burleigh Music Workshop and Music Ministry, Oklahoma City, OK
www.halleonard.com	Hal Leonard Publications, Milwaukee, WI
www.musicanet.org	MUSICA, Strasbourg, France
www.ocp.org	Oregon Catholic Press, Portland, OR

SELECTED BIBLIOGRAPHY

Abbington, James. *Let Mt. Zion Rejoice! Music in the African American Church.* Valley Forge, PA: Judson Press, 2001.

Abbington, James, editor. *Readings in African American Church Music and Worship.* Chicago: GIA Publications, Inc., 2001.

Aghahowa, Brenda Eatman. *Praising in Black and White: Unity and Diversity in Christian* Worship. Cleveland: United Church Press, 1996.

Bell, Derrick. *Gospel Choirs: Psalms of Survival in an Alien Land Called Home.* New York: Basic Books, 1996.

Bell, John L. *The Singing Thing: A Case for Congregational Song.* Chicago: GIA Publications, 2000.

Berglund, Brad. *Reinventing Sunday: Breakthrough Ideas for Transforming Worship.* Valley Forge, PA: Judson Press, 2001.

Berkley, James D., editor. *Leadership Handbook of Preaching and Worship.* Grand Rapids, MI: Baker Book House Co., 1992.

Borsch, Frederick Houk. *Introducing the Lessons of the Church Year: A Guide for Lay Readers and Congregations.* New York: Seabury Press, 1978.

Bower, Peter C., editor. *Handbook for the Revised Common Lectionary.* Louisville, KY: Westminster John Knox Press, 1996.

Boyer, Horace Clarence. *How Sweet the Sound: The Golden Age of Gospel.* Washington, DC: Elliott and Clark Publishing, 1995.

Causey, C. Harry. *Things They Didn't Tell Me About Being A Minister of Music.* Rockville, MD: Music Revelation, 1988.

Chapman, Mark L. *Christianity on Trial: African-American Religious Thought Before and After Black Power.* Maryknoll, NY: Orbis Books, 1996.

Cherwien, David M. *Let the People Sing!* St. Louis: Concordia Publishing House, 1997.

Cone, James H. *The Spiritual and the Blues.* Maryknoll, NY: Orbis Books, 1972.

Costen, Melva Wilson. *African American Christian Worship.* Nashville: Abingdon Press, 1993.

Davies, J. G., editor. *The New Westminster Dictionary of Liturgy and Worship.* Philadelphia: The Westminster Press, 1986.

Dawn, Marva J. *A Royal "Waste" of Time: The Splendor of Worshiping God and Being Church for the World.* Grand Rapids, MI: William B. Eerdmans Publishing Company, 1999.

Dawn, Marva J. *Reaching Out Without Dumbing Down: A Theology of Worship for the Turn of-the-Century Culture.* Grand Rapids, MI: William. B. Eerdmans Publishing Company, 1995.

DuBois, W.E.B. *The Souls of Black Folk.* New York: Dover Publications, 1994.

Dudley, Grenae D. and Carlyle F. Stewart III. *Sanfoka: Celebrations for the African-American Church.* Cleveland: United Church Press, 1997.

Dyson, Michael Eric. *Between God and Gangsta Rap: Bearing Witness to Black Culture.* New York: Oxford University Press, 1996.

Evans, Jr., James H. *We Have Been Believers: An African-American Systematic Theology.* Minneapolis: Fortress, 1992.

Evans, Jr., James H. *We Shall All Be Changed: Social Problems and Theological Renewal.* Minneapolis: Fortress, 1997.

Fisher, Miles Mark. *Negro Slave Songs in the United States.* New York: Citadel Press, 1953.

Floyd, Jr. Samuel A. *The Power of Black Music: Interpreting Its History from Africa to the United States.* New York: Oxford University Press, 1995.

Frame, John M. *Worship in Spirit and Truth: A Refreshing Study of the Principles and Practice of Biblical Worship.* Phillipsburg: P & R Publishing, 1996.

Franklin, Robert M. *Another Day's Journey: Black Churches Confronting the American Crisis.* Minneapolis: Fortress Press, 1997.

Goatley, David Emmanuel. *Were You There? Godforsakenness in Slave Religion.* Maryknoll, NY: Orbis Books, 1996.

Guimont, Michel. *Psalms for the Revised Common Lectionary.* Chicago: GIA Publications, Inc., 2000.

Harris, Michael W. *The Rise of Gospel Blues: The Music of Thomas Andrew* Dorsey *in the Urban Church.* New York: Oxford University Press, 1992.

Hickman, Hoyt L., Don E. Saliers, Laurence Hull Stokey, and James White. *The New Handbook of the Christian Year.* Nashville: Abingdon Press, 1992.

Holck, Jr., Manfred, compiler. *Dedication Services for Every Occasion.* Valley Forge, PA: Judson Press, 1984.

Holmes, Jr. Zan W. *Encountering Jesus.* Nashville: Abingdon Press, 1992.

Hollies, Linda H. *Trumpet in Zion: Worship Resources, Year A.* Cleveland: Pilgrim Press, 2001.

Hood, Robert E. *Begrimed and Black: Christian Traditions on Blacks and Blackness.* Minneapolis: Fortress Press, 1994.

Hood, Robert E. *Must God Remain Greek? Afro Cultures and God-talk.* Minneapolis: Fortress Press, 1990.

Hurston, Zola Neale. *The Sanctified Church.* Berkeley, CA: Turtle Island, 1981.

Jackson, Irene V., editor. *Afro-American Religious Music: A Bibliography and Catalogue of Gospel Music.* Westport, NY: Greenwood Press, 1979.

Jones, Arthur C. *Wade in the Water: The Wisdom on the Spirituals.* Maryknoll, NY: Orbis Books, 1993.

Jordan, James. *The Musician's Soul.* Chicago: GIA Publications, 1999.

Keener, Craig S. and Glenn Usry. *Defending Black Faith: Answers to Tough Questions about African-American Christianity.* Downers Grove, IL: Inter-Varsity Press, 1997.

Keikert, Patrick R. *Welcoming the Stranger: A Public Theology of Worship and Evangelism.* Minneapolis: Fortress Press, 1992.

Kirk-Duggan, Cheryl A. *African American Special Days: 15 Complete Worship Services.* Nashville: Abingdon Press, 1996.

Kirk-Duggan, Cheryl A. *Exorcizing Evil: A Womanist Perspective on the Spirituals.* Maryknoll, NY: Orbis Books, 1997.

Lehman, Victor. *The Pastor's Guide to Weddings and Funerals.* Valley Forge, PA: Judson Press, 2001.

Liesch, Barry. *The New Worship: Straight Talk on Music and the Church.* Grand Rapids, MI: Baker Book House Co., 1996.

Lincoln, C. Eric and Lawrence Mamiya. *The Black Church in the African American Experience.* Durham, NC: Duke University Press, 1990.

Lovell, Jr., John. *Black Song: The Forge and the Flame.* New York: Macmillan, 1972.

Mapson, Jr., J. Wendell. *The Ministry of Music in the Black Church.* Valley Forge, PA: Judson Press. 1984.

Mapson, Jr., J. Wendell. *Strange Fire: A Study of Worship and Liturgy in the African American Church.* St. Louis: Hodale Press, 1996.

McClain. William B. *Come Sunday: The Liturgy of Zion.* Nashville: Abingdon Press, 1990.

Mitchell, Robert H. *I Don't Like That Music.* Carol Steam, IL: Hope Publishing Company, 1993.

Moffett, Diane Givens. *Beyond Greens and Cornbread: Reflections on African American Christian Identity.* Valley Forge, PA: Judson Press, 2002.

Orr, N. Lee. *The Church Music Handbook for Pastors and Musicians.* Nashville: Abingdon Press, 1991.

Owens, Bill. *The Magnetic Music Ministry.* Nashville: Abingdon Press, 1996.

Pitts Jr., Walter F. *Old Ship of Zion: The Afro-Baptist Ritual in the African Diaspora.* New York: Oxford University Press, 1993.

Raboteau, Albert J. *Slave Religion: The "Invisible Institution" in the Antebellum South.* New York: Oxford University Press, 1978.

Raboteau, Robert J. *A Fire in the Bones: Reflections on African-American Religious History.* Boston: Beacon Press, 1995.

Reagon, Bernice Johnson, editor. *We'll Understand It Better By and By: Pioneering African-American Gospel Composers.* Washington, DC: Smithsonian Institution Press, 1992.

Sanders, Cheryl J. *Saints in Exile: The Holiness-Pentecostal Experience in African American Religion and Culture.* New York: Oxford University Press, 1996.

Southern, Eileen. *Readings in Black American Music.* New York: W. W. Norton and Company, 1971.

Southern, Eileen. *The Music of Black Americans: A History.* Third Edition. New York: W. W. Norton and Company, 1997.

Spencer, Donald A. *Hymn and Scripture Selection Guide: A Cross-Reference Tool for Worship Leaders.* Grand Rapids, MI: Baker Book House, 1993.

Spencer, Jon Michael. *Black Hymnody: A Hymnological History of the African-American Church.* Knoxville, TN: The University of Tennessee Press, 1992.

Spencer, Jon Michael. *Protest and Praise: Sacred Music of Black Religion.* Minneapolis: Fortress Press, 1990.

Spencer, Jon Michael. *Sing a New Song: Liberating Black Hymnody.* Minneapolis: Fortress Press, 1995.

Stewart III, Carlyle F. *Black Spirituality and Black Consciousness: Soul Force, Culture and Freedom in the African-American Experience.* Trenton, NJ: Africa World Press, 1999.

Stewart III, Carlyle F. *Soul Survivors: An African American Spirituality.* Louisville: Westminster John Knox Press, 1997.

Stewart III, Carlyle F. *African American Church Growth: 12 Principles for Prophetic Ministry.* Nashville: Abingdon Press, 1994.

Talbot, Frederick H. *African American Worship: New Eyes for Seeing.* Lima, OH: Fairway Press, 1998.

The Revised Common Lectionary: The Consultation on Common Texts. Nashville: Abingdon Press, 1992.

Walker, Wyatt Tee. *Somebody's Calling My Name: Black Sacred Music and Social Change.* Valley Forge, PA: Judson Press, 1979.

Warren, Gwendolin Sims. *Ev'ry Time I Feel the Spirit: 101 Best-Loved Psalms, Gospel Hymns, and Spiritual Songs of the African-American Church.* New York: Henry Holt and Company, 1997.

Washington, James Melvin. *Conversations With God. Two Centuries of Prayers by African Americans.* New York: HarperCollins Publishers, 1994.

Webber, Robert E. *Worship is a Verb: Eight Principles for Transforming Worship.* Second Edition. Peabody, MA: Hendrickson Publishers, 1995.

Webber, Robert. *Planning Blended Worship: The Creative Mixture of Old and New.* Nashville: Abingdon Press, 1998.

Westermeyer, Paul. *Te Deum: The Church and Music.* Minneapolis: Fortress, 1998.

Westermeyer, Paul. *With Tongues of Fire: Profiles in 20th-Century Hymn Writing.* St. Louis: Concordia Publishing House, 1995.

Wilmore, Gayraud S. *Last Things First: Library of Living Faith.* Philadelphia: The Westminster Press, 1982,

Wimbush, Vincent L., editor. *African Americans and The Bible: Sacred Texts and Social Textures.* New York: Continuum International Publishing Group, 2000.

Wright, Jr. Jeremiah A. *Africans Who Shaped the Faith: A Study of 10 Biblical Personalities.* Chicago: Urban Ministries, 1995.